T0085575

Chopin
2010

WYDANIE NARODOWE
DZIEŁ FRYDERYKA CHOPINA

NATIONAL EDITION
OF THE WORKS OF FRYDERYK CHOPIN

POLONAISES
PUBLISHED POSTHUMOUSLY

NATIONAL EDITION
Edited by JAN EKIER

PWM EDITION

SERIES B. WORKS PUBLISHED POSTHUMOUSLY. VOLUME II

FRYDERYK CHOPIN

POLONEZY

WYDANE POŚMIERTNIE

WYDANIE NARODOWE
Redaktor naczelny: JAN EKIER

FUNDACJA WYDANIA NARODOWEGO
POLSKIE WYDAWNICTWO MUZYCZNE SA
WARSZAWA 2019

SERIA B. UTWORY WYDANE POŚMIERTNIE. TOM II

Redakcja tomu: Jan Ekier, Paweł Kamiński

Komentarz wykonawczy i Komentarz źródłowy (skrócony) dołączone są do nut głównej serii *Wydania Narodowego* oraz do strony internetowej www.chopin-nationaledition.com

Pełne *Komentarze źródłowe* do poszczególnych tomów będą publikowane oddzielnie.

Wydany w oddzielnym tomie *Wstęp do Wydania Narodowego Dzieł Fryderyka Chopina – 1. Zagadnienia edytorskie* obejmuje całokształt ogólnych problemów wydawniczych, zaś *Wstęp... – 2. Zagadnienia wykonawcze* – całokształt ogólnych problemów interpretacyjnych. Pierwsza część *Wstępu* jest także dostępna na stronie www.pwm.com.pl

Polonezy przygotowane do druku i wydane przez Chopina zawarte są w osobnym tomie 6 **A VI**.

Editors of this Volume: Jan Ekier, Paweł Kamiński

A *Performance Commentary* and a *Source Commentary (abridged)* are included in the music of the main series of the *National Edition* and available on www.chopin-nationaledition.com

Full *Source Commentaries* on each volume will be published separately.

The *Introduction to the National Edition of the Works of Fryderyk Chopin*
1. Editorial Problems, published as a separate volume, covers general matters concerning the publication.
The *Introduction... 2. Problems of Performance* covers all general questions of the interpretation.
First part of the *Introduction* is also available on the website www.pwm.com.pl

The *Polonaises* prepared for print and published by Chopin are contained in a separate volume 6 **A VI**.

Polonez B-dur / Polonaise in B♭ major, WN 1
page / s. 12
1
Polonez g-moll / Polonaise in G minor, WN 2
page / s. 14
2
Polonez As-dur / Polonaise in A♭ major, WN 3
page / s. 16
3
Polonez gis-moll / Polonaise in G♯ minor, WN 4
page / s. 19
4
dolce con grazia
Polonez b-moll / Polonaise in B♭ minor, WN 10
page / s. 24
5
mezza voce
Polonez d-moll / Polonaise in D minor, WN 11
page / s. 28
6
a tempo
Polonez f-moll / Polonaise in F minor, WN 12
page / s. 34
7
espressivo
Polonez B-dur / Polonaise in B♭ major, WN 17
page / s. 40
8
sempre tranquillamente
Polonez Ges-dur / Polonaise in G♭ major, WN 35
page / s. 46
9
dolce
DODATEK / APPENDIX
Wcześniejsze wersje / Earlier versions
Polonez As-dur / Polonaise in A♭ major, WN 3
page / s. 55
(3)
Polonez f-moll / Polonaise in F minor, WN 12
page / s. 58
(7)
espress.
ten.

o Polonezach ...

WN 2

„[...] przemilczeć [...] przed publicznością nie możemy kompozycji następującej, przez przyjacielskie ręce sztychem upowszechnionej: Polonaise pour Pianoforte dédiée à son Excellence Mlle la Comtesse Victoire Skarbek par Frédéric Chopin agé de 8 ans. Kompozytor tego tańca Polskiego, młodzieniec ośm dopiero lat skończonych mający, [...] prawdziwy geniusz muzyczny: nie tylko bowiem z łatwością największą i smakiem nadzwyczajnym wygrywa sztuki najtrudniejsze na fortepianie, ale nad to jest już kompozytorem kilku tańców i wariacji, nad którymi znawcy muzyki dziwić się nie przestają, a nade wszystko zważając na wiek dziecinny autora."

Fragment wzmianki w „Pamiętniku Warszawskim", r. IV, tom X, 1818.

WN 4

„O ile z manuskryptu i dedykacji wnosić można, kompozycja ta napisaną została w 14 roku życia przez Fryderyka Chopin, i nigdzie dotychczas drukowaną nie była."

Notka pod pierwszą stroną tekstu nutowego polskiego pierwodruku J. Kaufmanna, Warszawa 1864.

WN 10

„Przesyłam Panom dzisiaj jeden Polonez i jeden Mazurek. Poloneza nie dało się odnaleźć po śmierci mego brata w 1877 r. w pozostawionych papierach; przypominam sobie, że miał nawet dwa jego egzemplarze, mianowicie brudnopis i staranniej napisany tekst; skopiowałem go według tego ostatniego przed około 18 laty i podaję tutaj odpis tegoż."

Z listu Oskara Kolberga do firmy Breitkopf i Härtel w Lipsku, Kraków 3 XII 1878.

„Co do poloneza Szopena [...] to tyle tylko powiedzieć mogę, że był on dedykowany memu bratu Wilhelmowi, koledze szkolnemu Fryderyka [...] Napisany był przed samym wyjazdem Fryd[eryka] do Reinerz w r. 1826; w wilię dnia tego obadwaj byli na przedstawieniu Sroki-złodziej w teatrze (czy też może na prywatnym wieczorku arię z niej słyszeli, czego nie pamiętam) – a że się melodia ta bratu bardzo podobała, przeto ją Sz[open] wpakował do tria."

Z listu Oskara Kolberga do Jana Kleczyńskiego w Warszawie, Kraków 23 V 1881.

WN 12

„Nie mogłem się wymówić od przysłania im [ks. Radziwiłłom z Antonina] Poloneza mojego f-minor, który zajął X-czkę Elizę, proszę Cię więc przyszlij mi go najpierwszą pocztą, bo nie chcę być poczytanym za niegrzecznego, a z pamięci pisać nie chcę, kochanku, bobym inaczej może napisał, aniżeli jest w istocie. — Możesz sobie wystawić charakter X-czki, kiedy jej co dzień tego Poloneza grać musiałem, i nic tak nie lubiła jak to Trio As-dur. [...] Jeszcze ci raz przypominam Poloneza f-minor, przyślij mi go, moje życie, pierwszą pocztą."

Z listu F. Chopina do Tytusa Woyciechowskiego w Poturzynie, Warszawa 14 XI 1829.

WN 35

„[...] Polonez wcale znakomity, wypisany snać ukradkiem z albumu p. Tyt[usa] Woyciechowskiego i wydany w Warszawie u Kaufmanna [...]"

Z uwag Oskara Kolberga do pracy Maurycego Antoniego Szulca o Chopinie, dołączonych do listu z 13 XI 1874.

„Drugą prośbą jest odszukanie Poloneza Szopena z Ges-dur, wydanego [...] przed 20 laty przez Kaufmanna (jako Polonez sławnego artysty, zmarłego niedawno w Paryżu) i w drugiej edycji także, a którego ja i po albumach przepisanego widywałem."

Z listu Oskara Kolberga do Józefa Sikorskiego [w Zakopanem], [Modlnica] 27 IX 1879.

„Chwila, w której dzieła Chopina staną się wspólną własnością, jest coraz bliższa i musimy ze wszystkich sił dążyć do tego, by zamknąć spis utworów. Dużą trudność sprawia nam spuścizna utworów fortepianowych tomu XIII, w którym brak jeszcze wciąż podkładów do Mazurka a-moll nr 13 i Poloneza Ges-dur nr 21, co szczególnie hamuje przygotowanie naszych palcowanych wydań."

Z listu Breitkopfa i Härtla do Oskara Kolberga w Modlnicy, Lipsk 9 X 1879.

„Chodzi mi szczególnie o Poloneza, którego przed kilkunastu laty widywałem w albumach kilku dam w Warsz[awie] i mówiono mi, że pochodzi od Sz[anownego] Pana; dziś edycja Kaufmanna jest wyczerpana i trudno mi tego dostać. Prosiłbym o łaskawą jego kopię [...]."

Z listu Oskara Kolberga do Tytusa Woyciechowskiego [adresat zmarł 9 miesięcy przed napisaniem tego listu], Modlnica 15 XII 1879.

„[... Polonez] Ges-dur, który się znajdował w Oeuvres posthumes (w liczbie 6), jakie wydał był Kaufmann, poprzednio zaś, jako Polonez sławnego artysty zmarłego w Paryżu, był on przezeń publikowany oddzielnie. Sam ja kilka egzemplarzy jego miałem w swoim czasie w ręku; dziś atoli brak mi go do kompletu. W przypuszczeniu, że go znasz lub pozyskać możesz, prosiłbym Szan[ownego] Pana o nadesłanie mi jego odpisu [...]"

Z listu Oskara Kolberga do Jana Kleczyńskiego w Warszawie, Kraków 2 VI 1880.

„Polonez Chopina od dawna już przepisany posyłam Panu nareszcie."

Z listu Jana Kleczyńskiego do Oskara Kolberga w Krakowie, Warszawa 20 IX 1880.

„Mam przyjemność przesłać Panom w załączeniu najlepszą wersję kursującego w odpisach Poloneza Ges-dur Chopina. [...] Polonez ten znany był pod nazwą «Pożegnanie Warszawy w roku 1830» (Les adieux de Varsovie). Chopin napisał go krótko przed wyjazdem za granicę, tylko dla zażyłych przyjaciół i współuczniów i nie myślał za życia o jego opublikowaniu [...]."

Z listu Oskara Kolberga do firmy Breitkopf i Härtel w Lipsku, Kraków 5 I 1881.

„Co się tyczy [...] Poloneza Ges-dur Chopina, braliśmy sami pod uwagę włączenie go do wydania zbiorowego, ostateczną decyzję pozostawiając redakcji, wypadła ona niestety odmownie."

Z listu Breitkopfa i Härtla do Oskara Kolberga w Krakowie, Lipsk 15 V 1885.

„Polonez Ges-dur [...], pochodzący z młodych lat mistrza, wykazuje wszelkie cechy jego geniuszu. Dzieło to, które dał nam do dyspozycji p. A. Poliński, nie jest autografem, lecz kopią sporządzoną ręką przyjaciela młodości Chopina, Oskara Kolberga, słynnego etnografa [...]."

Z noty czasopisma „Die Musik", Chopin-Heft, rok VIII (1908/1909), Heft 1, do którego dołączony został drukowany tekst *Poloneza*.

about the Polonaises ...

WN 2

'[...] we cannot conceal [...] from the public the following composition, disseminated in print by the hand of a friend: Polonaise pour Pianoforte dédiée à son Excellence Mlle la Comtesse Victoire Skarbek par Frédéric Chopin agé de 8 ans. The composer of this Polish dance, a young lad only eight years of age [...] a true musical genius: not only does he play on the piano the most difficult pieces with the greatest facility and extraordinary taste, but he is already the composer of a number of dances and variations by which connoisseurs of music are unceasingly amazed, above all given their composer's youthful age.'

From a piece in the *Pamiętnik Warszawski*, year 4, vol. 10 (1818).

WN 4

'As far as one may deduce from the manuscript and its dedication, this composition was written by Fryderyk Chopin in his 14th year, and has not been previously printed anywhere.'

Note beneath the first page of the musical text of the Polish first edition, published by J. Kaufmann, Warsaw 1864.

WN 10

'I send you today one Polonaise and one Mazurka. The Polonaise could not be found after my brother's death in 1877 among the papers he left; I recall that he even had two copies, namely a working copy and a more meticulously written text; I copied it out from the latter some 18 years ago, and I present here a copy of it.'

From a letter sent by Oskar Kolberg to the firm of Breitkopf & Härtel in Leipzig, Kraków 3 Dec. 1878.

'As for Chopin's polonaise [...] I can say no more than this – that it was dedicated to my brother, Wilhelm, a school friend of Fryderyk [...] It was written just before Fryd[eryk] left for Reinerz in 1826; the previous day, the two of them had been to a production of "La gazza ladra" at the theatre (or possibly they heard an aria from it at a private soirée that I don't recall), and since my brother took a liking to this melody, Ch[opin] stuffed it in the trio.'

From a letter sent by Oskar Kolberg to Jan Kleczyński in Warsaw, Kraków 23 May 1881.

WN 12

'I couldn't get out of sending them [The Duke and Duchess Radziwiłł of Antonin] my F minor Polonaise, which entranced the Duchess Eliza, so I entreat you to send it to me by the very next post, as I don't wish to be seen as impolite, and I don't want to write it from memory, dear thing, because I might write it differently to how it actually looks. You can imagine the Duchess's character, when I had to play her this Polonaise every day, and she liked nothing better than the Trio in A♭ major. [...] Let me remind you once again, the Polonaise in F minor, send it to me, dear friend, by the earliest post.'

From a letter sent by Fryderyk Chopin to Tytus Woyciechowski in Poturzyn, Warsaw 14 Nov. 1829.

WN 35

'[...] An utterly brilliant Polonaise, presumably poached from the album of Mr Tyt[us] Woyciechowski and published by Kaufmann of Warsaw [...]'

From comments made by Oskar Kolberg on Maurycy Antoni Szulc's work on Chopin, attached to a letter from 13 Nov. 1874.

'My other request is that you search for Chopin's Polonaise in G♭ major, published [...] 20 years ago by Kaufmann (as a Polonaise by the famous musical artist recently deceased in Paris) and also as a second edition, and which I also saw written out in albums.'

From a letter sent by Oskar Kolberg to Józef Sikorski [in Zakopane], [Modlnica] 27 Sept. 1879.

'The moment when Chopin's works become common property is ever nearer and we must put all our energies into completing the list of his works. We are having considerable difficulty with the legacy of piano works from volume 12, in which we are still lacking base texts for the Mazurka in A minor, No. 13, and the Polonaise in G♭ major, No. 21, which is particularly hampering the preparation of our fingered editions.'

From a letter sent by Breitkopf & Härtel to Oskar Kolberg in Modlnica, Leipzig 9 Oct. 1879.

'I refer in particular to the Polonaise, which I saw 10-20 years ago in the albums of several ladies in Warsz[awa] and was told that it came from yourself; the Kaufmann edition is now out of print and difficult to get hold of. I would ask you kindly for a copy [...].'

From a letter sent by Oskar Kolberg to Tytus Woyciechowski [who died 9 months before this letter was written], Modlnica 15 Dec. 1879.

'[... The Polonaise] in G♭ major that appeared in the Oeuvres posthumes (6 in total) published by Kaufmann, who had previously published it separately as a Polonaise by the celebrated musical artist who died in Paris. I myself had several copies in my hand at one time or another; now, however, I need it for the complete set. Presuming that you know it or are able to acquire it, I would ask if you could kindly send me a copy [...]'

From a letter sent by Oskar Kolberg to Jan Kleczyński in Warsaw, Kraków 2 June 1880.

'I send you, finally, the Chopin Polonaise, long since copied out.'

From a letter by Jan Kleczyński to Oskar Kolberg in Kraków, Warsaw 20 Sept. 1880.

'It is my pleasure to enclose the best version of the Chopin Polonaise in G♭ major circulating in various copies. [...] This polonaise was known under the name "Farewell to Warsaw in 1830" (Les adieux de Varsovie). Chopin wrote it shortly before leaving the country, solely for close friends and fellow students, and had not thought of publishing it while alive [...].'

From a letter sent by Oskar Kolberg to the firm of Breitkopf & Härtel in Leipzig, Kraków 5 Jan. 1881.

'As regards [...] Chopin's Polonaise in G♭ major, we ourselves considered including it in the collected edition, leaving the final decision to the editors; this was unfortunately negative.'

From a letter sent by Breitkopf & Härtel to Oskar Kolberg in Kraków, Leipzig 15 May 1885.

'The Polonaise in G♭ major [...], dating from the master's youth, displays all the hallmarks of his genius. This work, made available to us by Mr A. Poliński, is not an autograph but a copy produced by the hand of a friend from Chopin's youth, the famous ethnographer Oskar Kolberg [...].'

From a note in the periodical *Die Musik*, Chopin-Heft, year 8 (1908/1909), Heft 1, to which the printed text of the Polonaise was attached.

Polonoise

WN 1

1

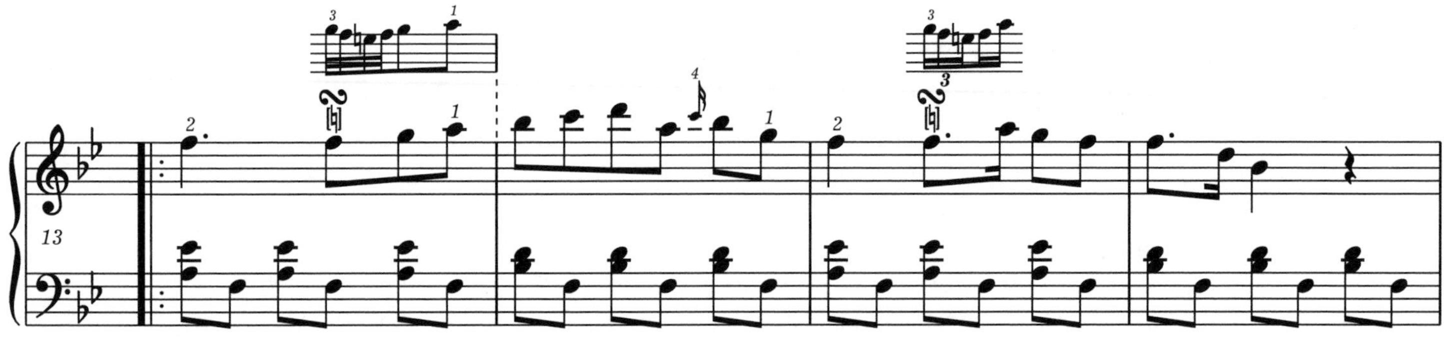

[Fine]

* (z wyjątkiem t. 19).
(except bar 19).

** Na dodanych pięcioliniach podane są rozwiązania ozdobników.
Given on additional staffs is the execution of ornaments.

TRIO

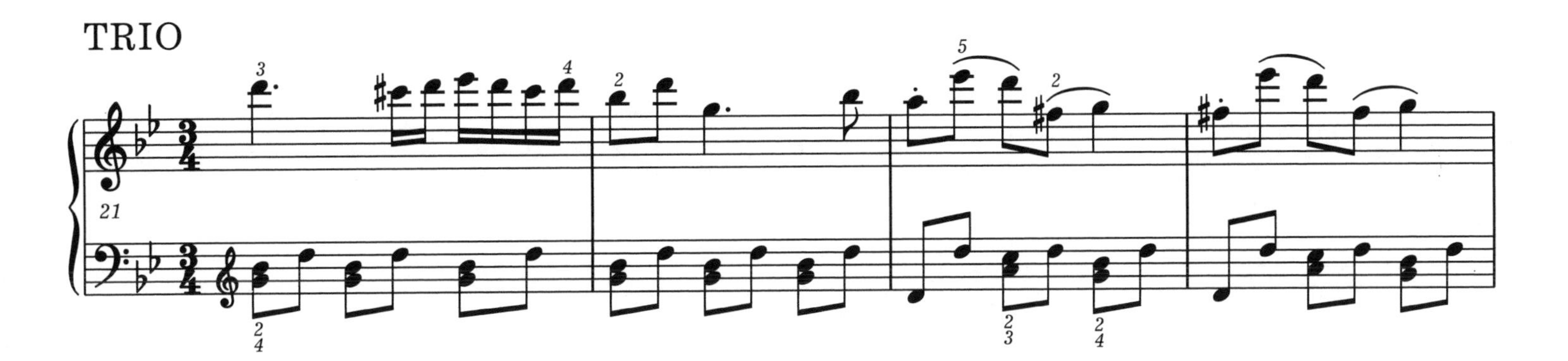

[Polonoise da Capo al Fine senza repetizioni]

* Wykonanie jak w t. 32.
To be executed as in bar 32.

Polonoise

A Son Excellence Mademoiselle la Comtesse Victoire Skarbek

WN 2

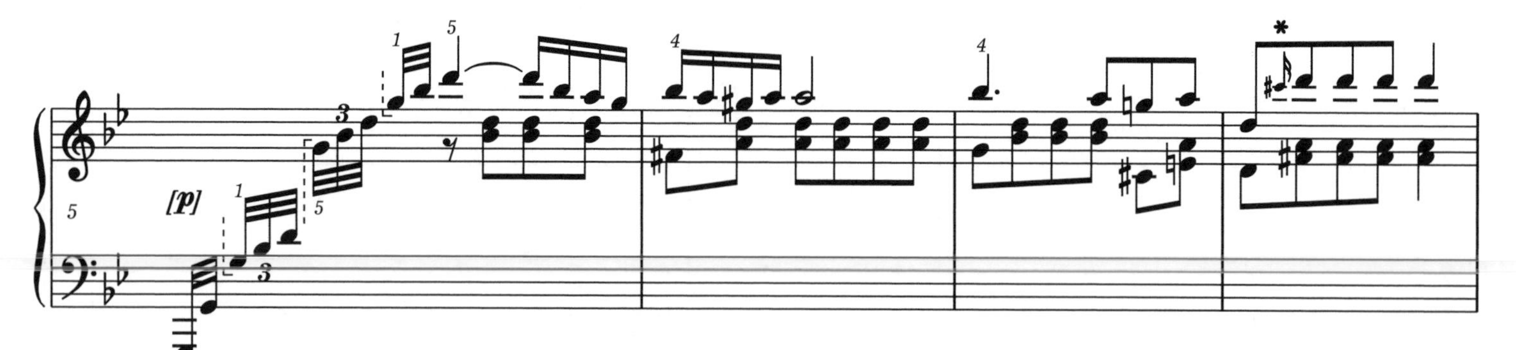

* ♪=♪

** Na dodanych pięcioliniach podane są rozwiązania ozdobników.
Given on additional staffs is the execution of ornaments.

*** Inna wersja taktu 22: Another version of bar 22 is  i jej wykonanie: , to be executed:

TRIO

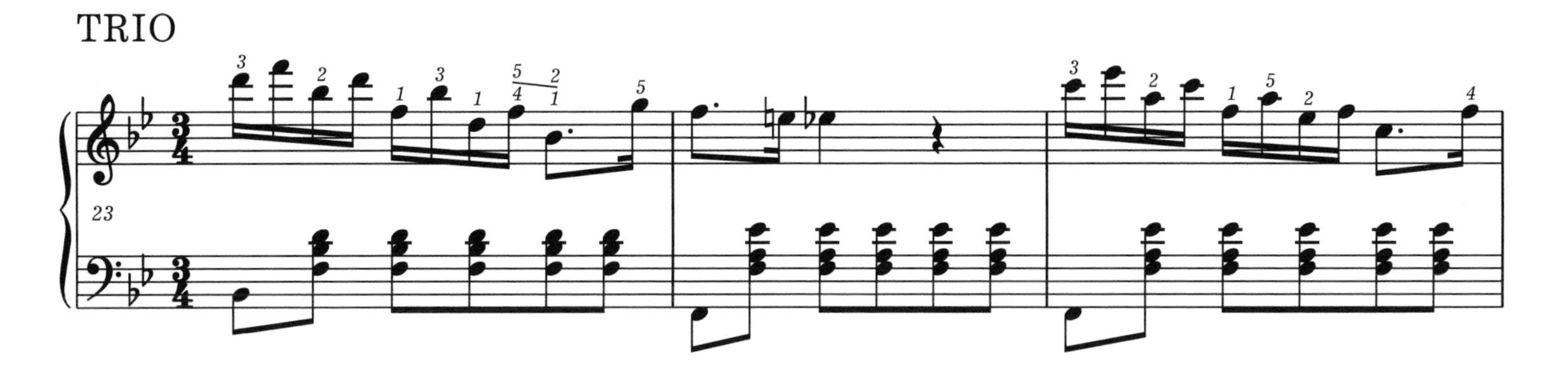

[Polonoise da Capo al Fine senza repetizione]

* Wykonanie jak w t. 29-30.
To be executed as in bars 29-30.

Polonaise

A Monsieur A. ywny

WN 3

* Patrz uwaga na następnej stronie.
Vide note on the next page.

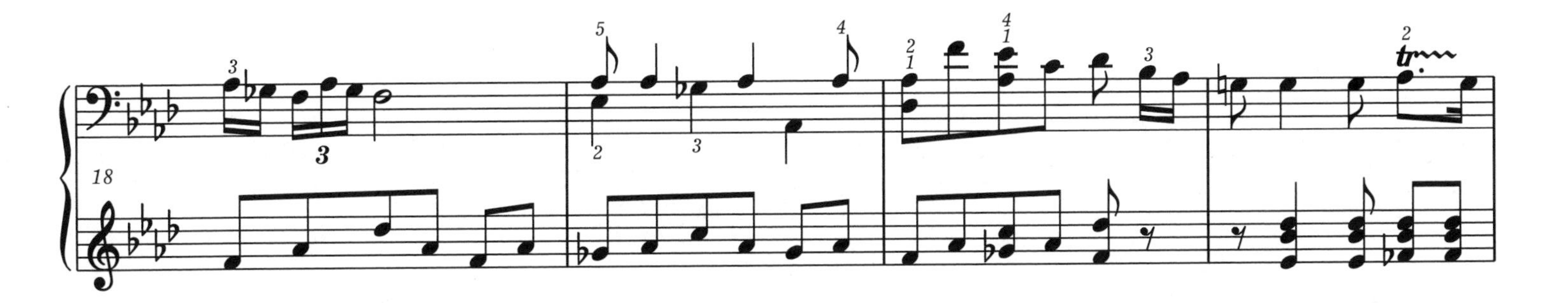

* Z autografu nie wynika jasno, czy Chopin chciał powtórzenia t. 13-38. Repetycję mo na traktować jako wariant.
It is not clear from the autograph whether Chopin wanted bars 13-38 to be repeated. The repetition can be treated as a variant.

TRIO

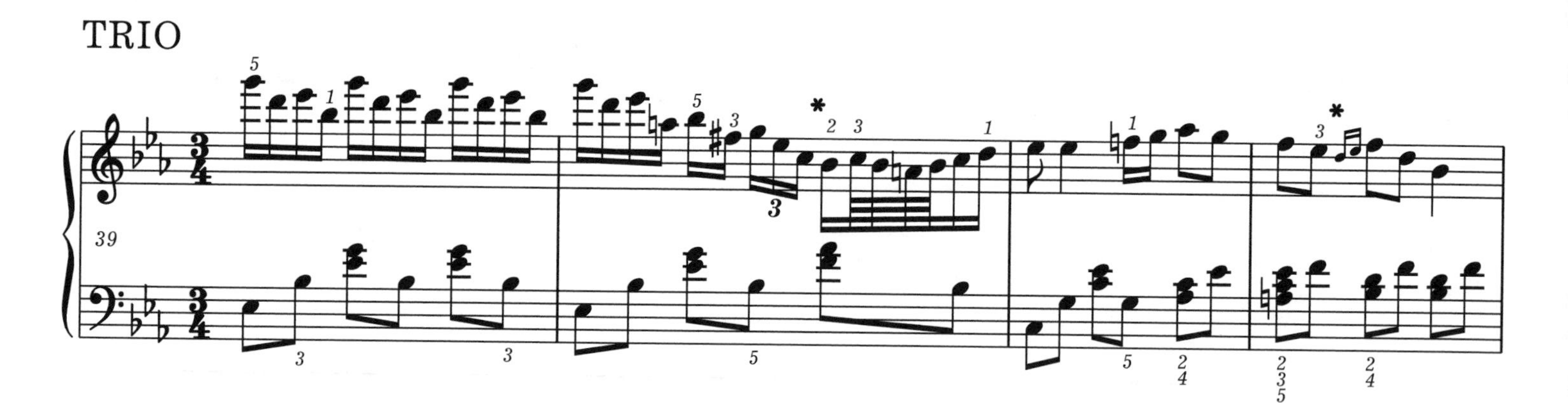

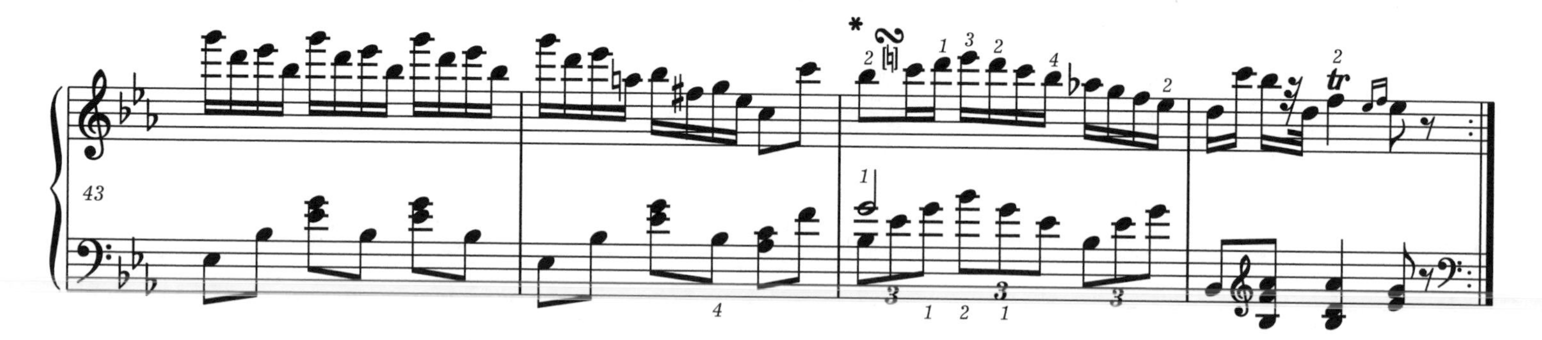

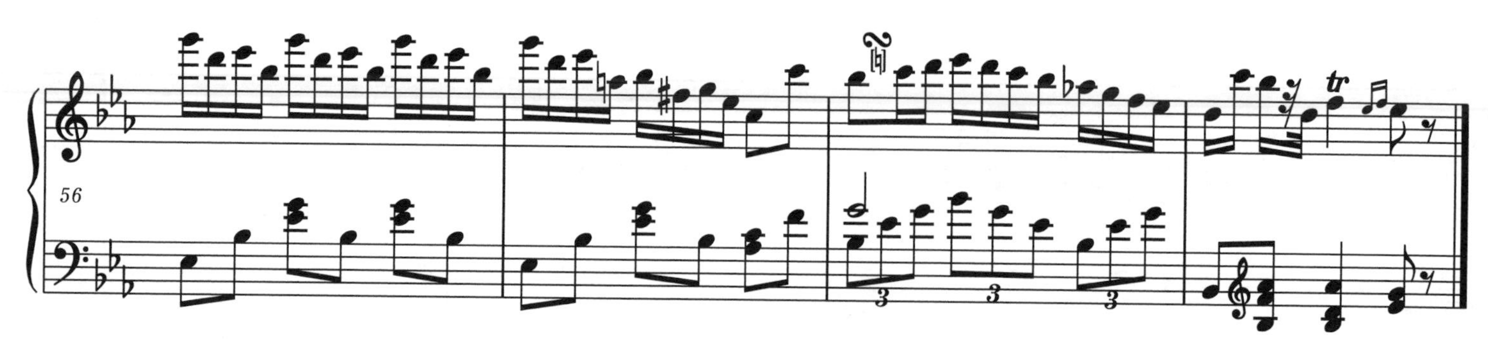

[Polonaise da Capo al Fine
senza repetizioni]

* Patrz *Komentarz wykonawczy.*
Vide *Performance Commentary.*

Polonaise *A Madame Du-Pont*

POLONEZ

WN 4

4

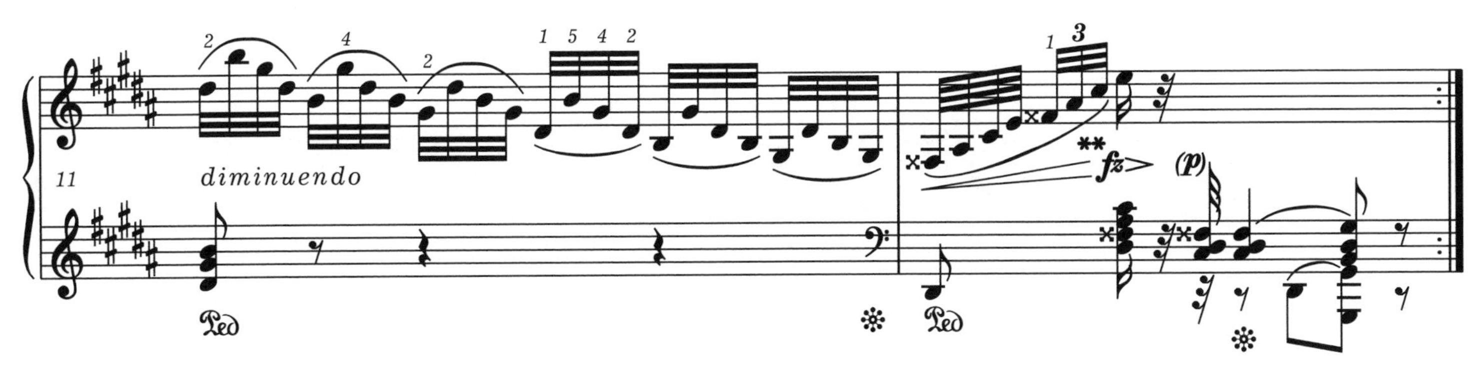

* Autentyczność wszelkich oznaczeń wykonawczych nie jest pewna. Patrz *Komentarz wykonawczy*.
There is uncertainty as to the authenticity of all performance markings. Vide *Performance Commentary*.

** Patrz *Komentarz źródłowy*.
Vide *Source Commentary*.

13
espressivo
Ped

16
8
p

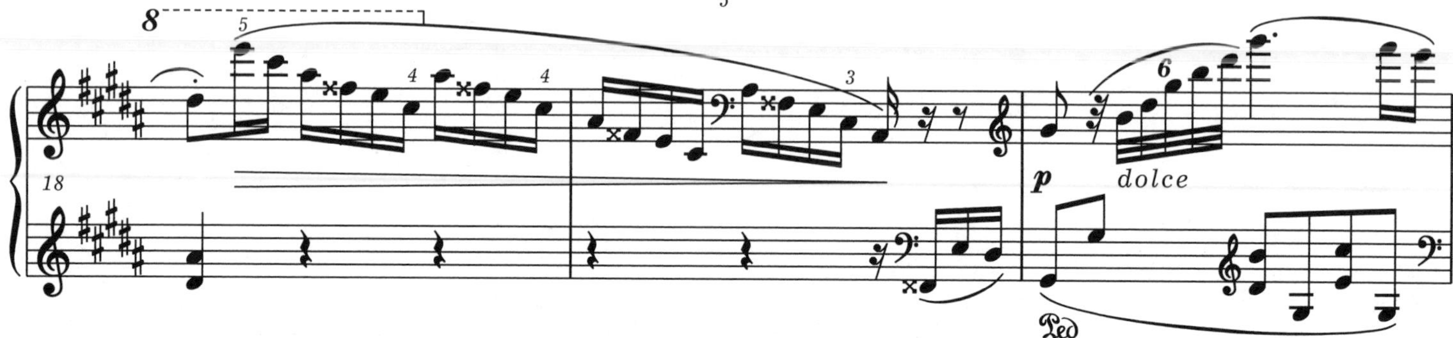
18
8
p
dolce
Ped

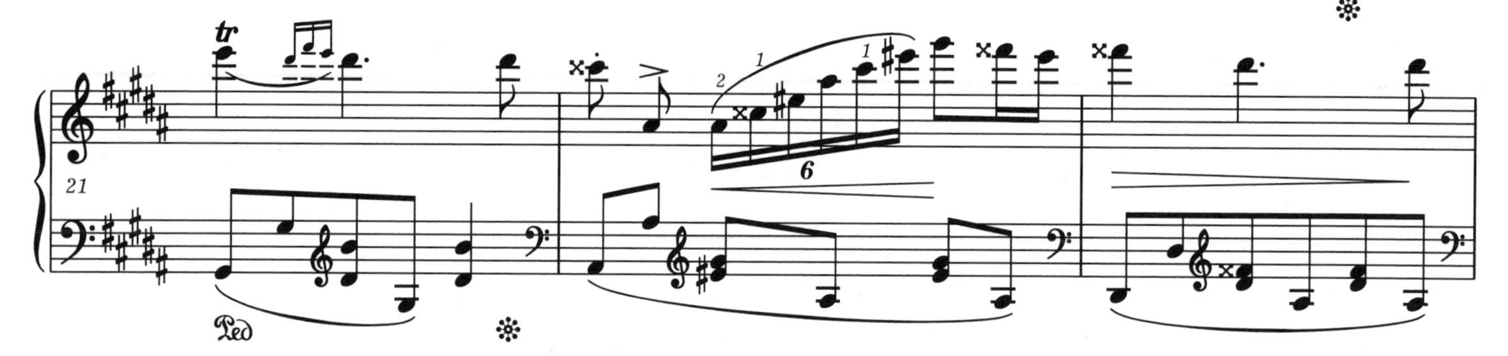
21
tr
Ped

24
8
p
f

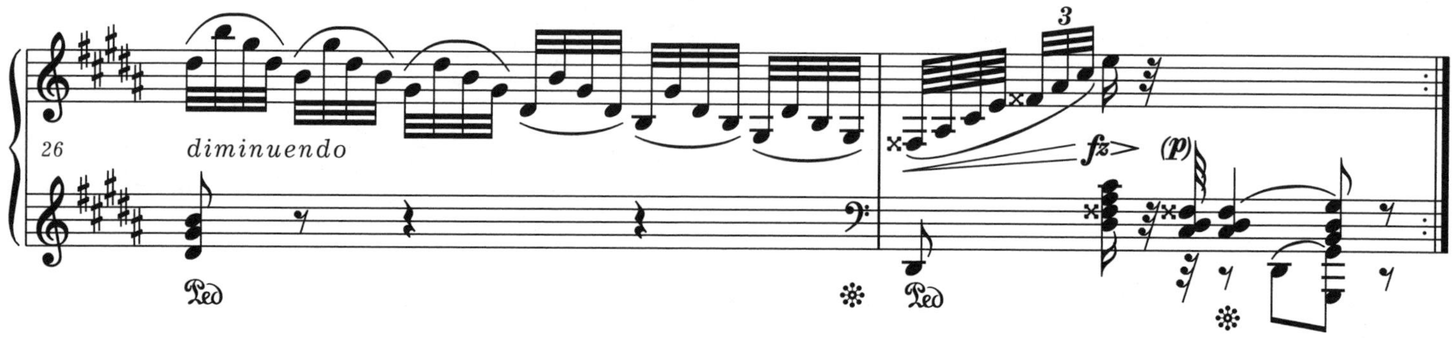
26
diminuendo
Ped
fz
(p)
Ped

[Fine]

TRIO

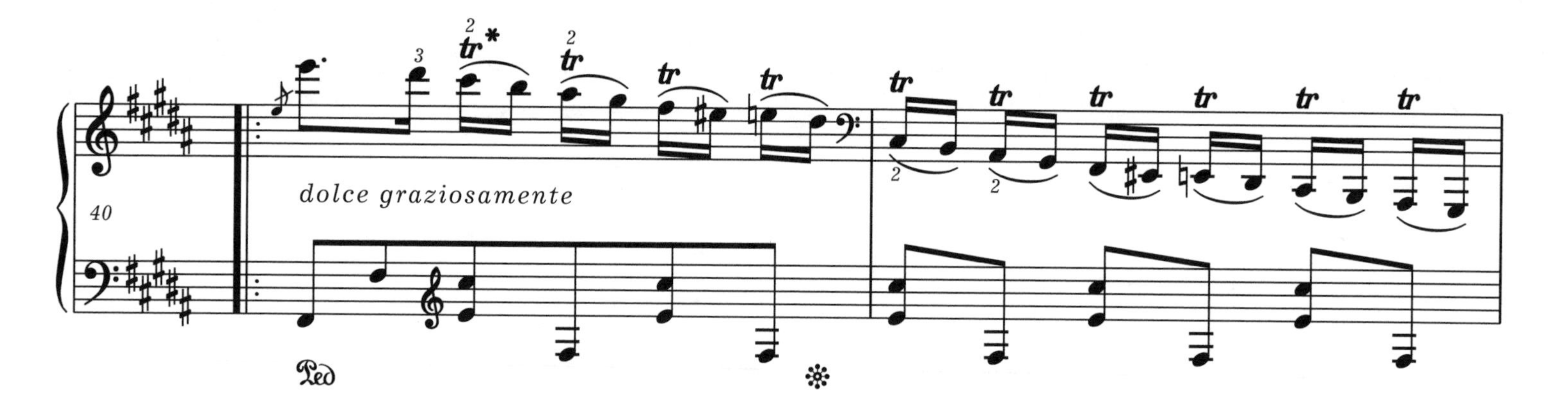
40
dolce graziosamente
Ped

42
Ped

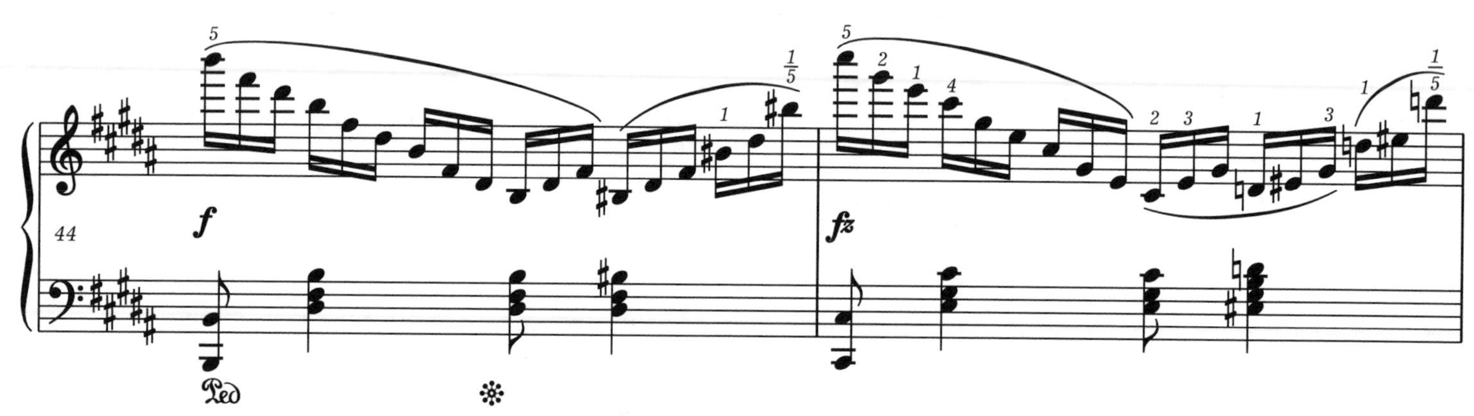
44
f
fz
Ped

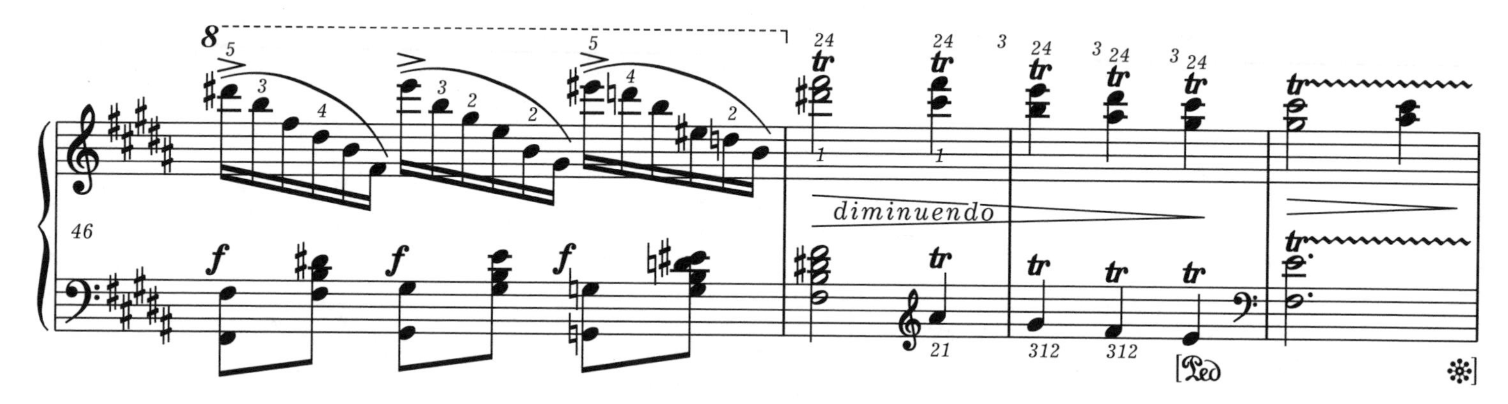
46
f
f
f
diminuendo
[Ped

50
p
Ped

* tr = 𝆖

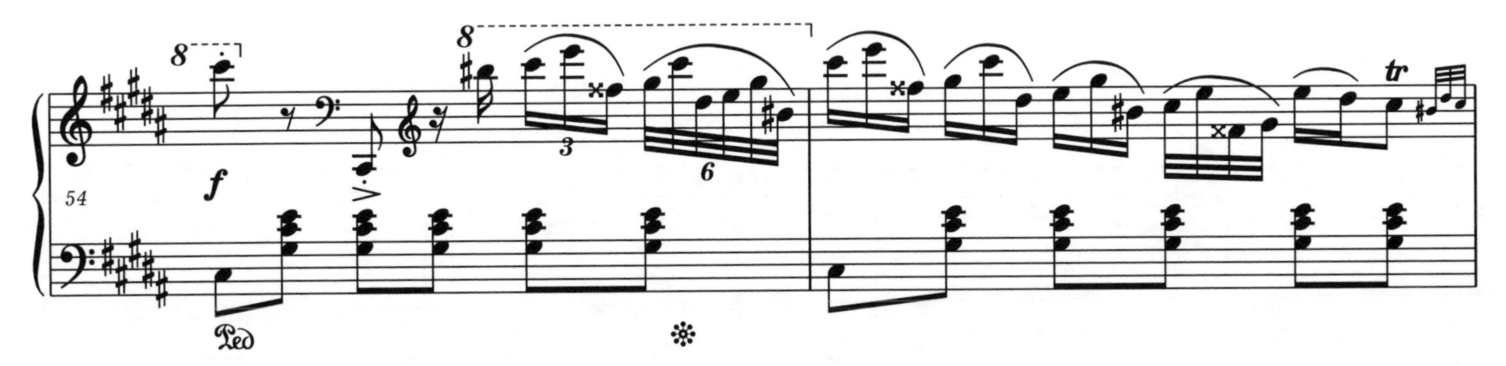

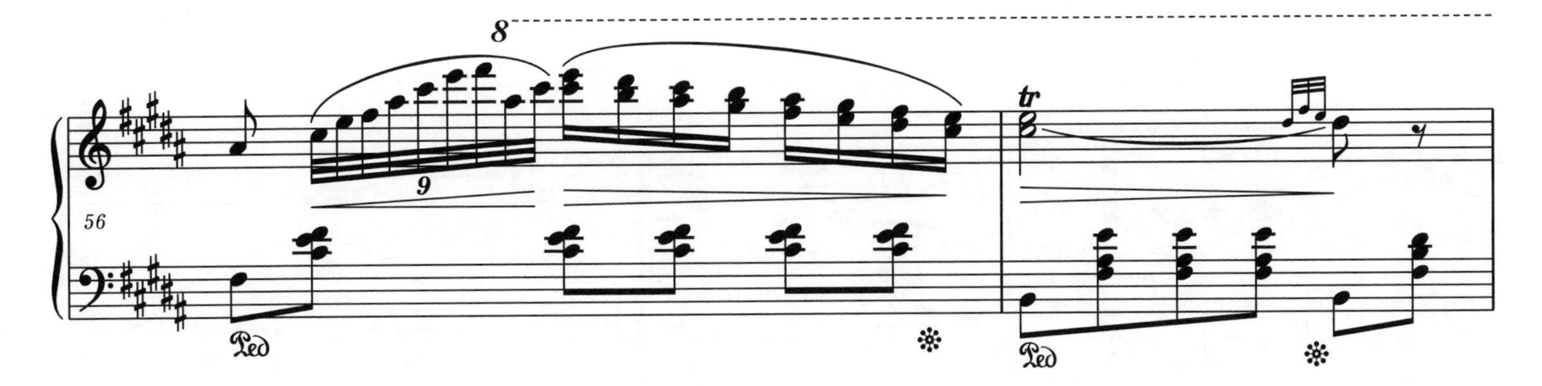

Polonez da Capo [al Fine
senza repetizioni]

Polonaise

Adieu à Guillaume Kolberg (en partant pour Reinerz)

WN 10

5

* tr = ∿∿

* lub ∾
or [♮]

* Au revoir!

TRIO tiré d'un air de la *Gazza ladra* par Rossini.

* Do widzenia! Trio według arii ze *Sroki złodziejki* Rossiniego.
Au revoir! A trio drawn from an aria from Rossini's *La gazza ladra*.

** **tr** = 𝆖

[Polonaise da Capo al Fine senza repetizione]

Polonaise

WN 11

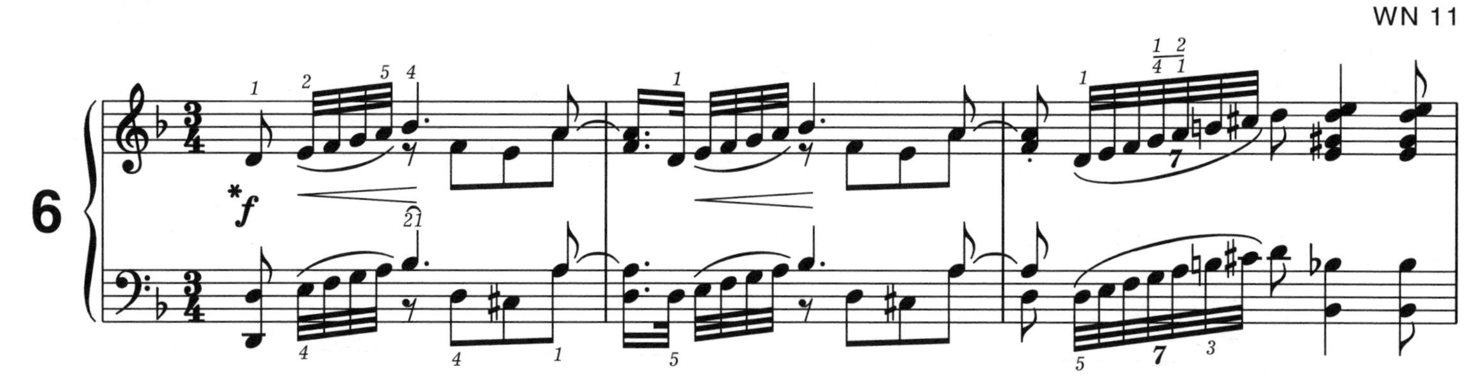

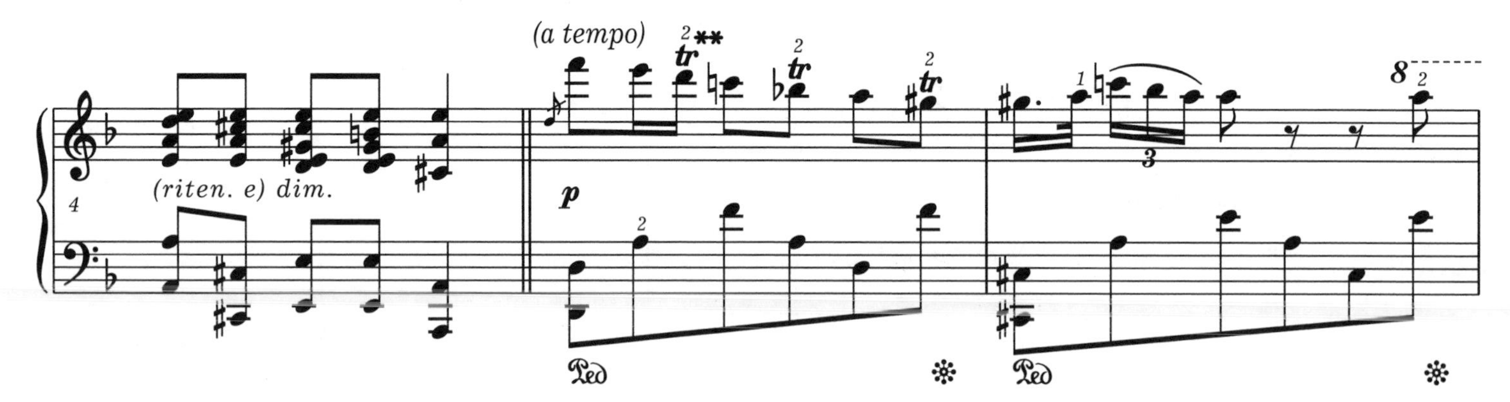

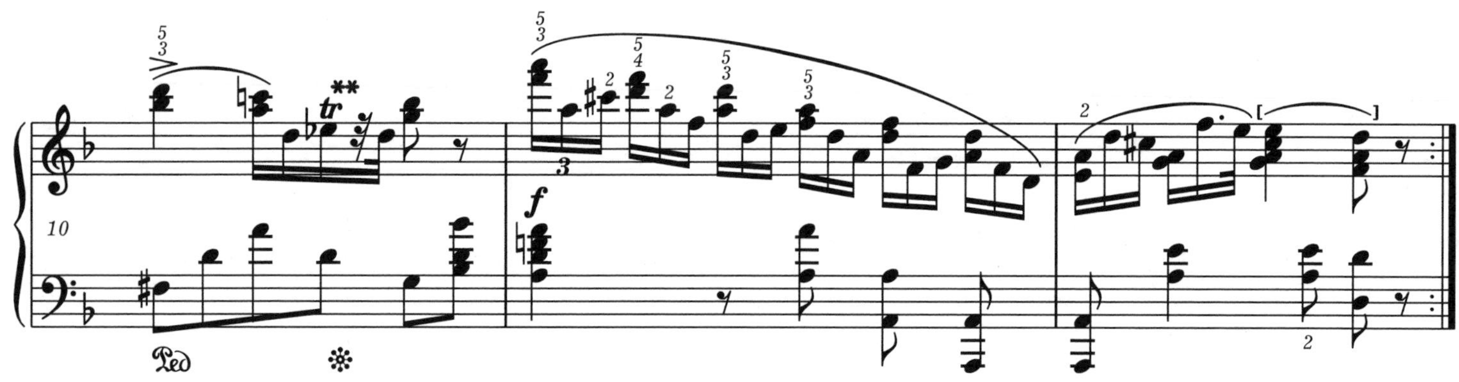

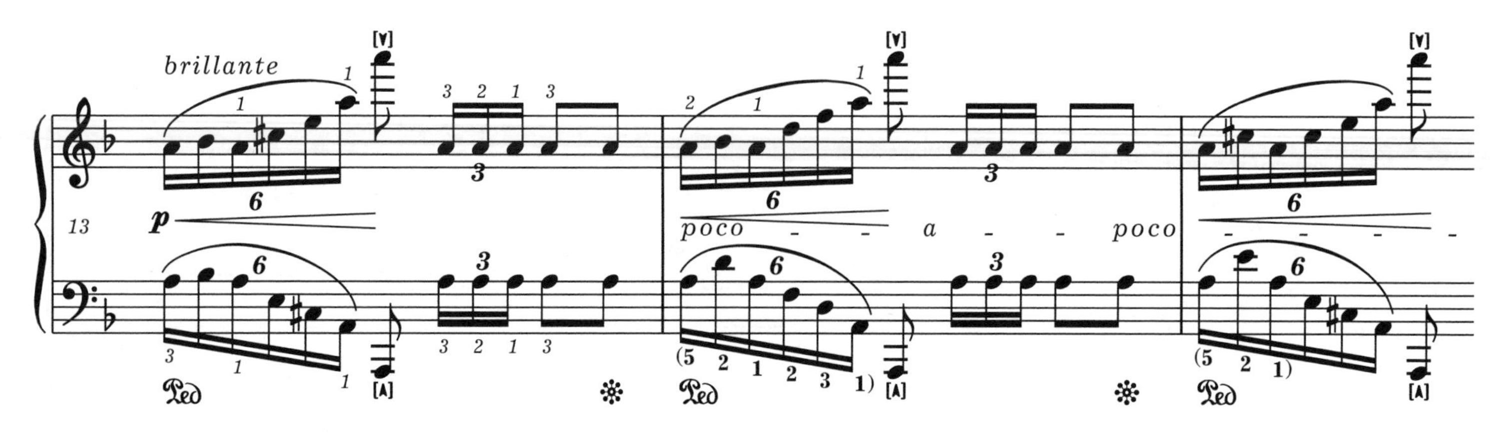

* Autentyczność wszelkich oznaczeń wykonawczych nie jest pewna. Patrz *Komentarz wykonawczy.*
There is uncertainty as to the authenticity of all performance markings. Vide *Performance Commentary.*

** **tr** nad szesnastką = 𝆖.
tr above a semiquaver = 𝆖.

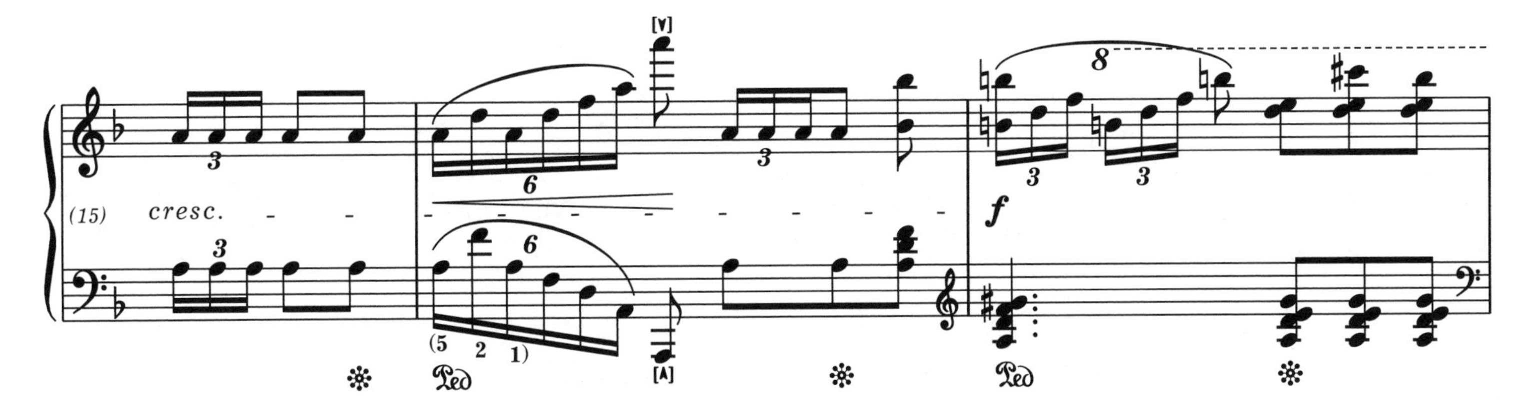
(15)
cresc.
f
Ped
Ped

18
Ped
Ped

20
p

22
f

24
p
cresc.

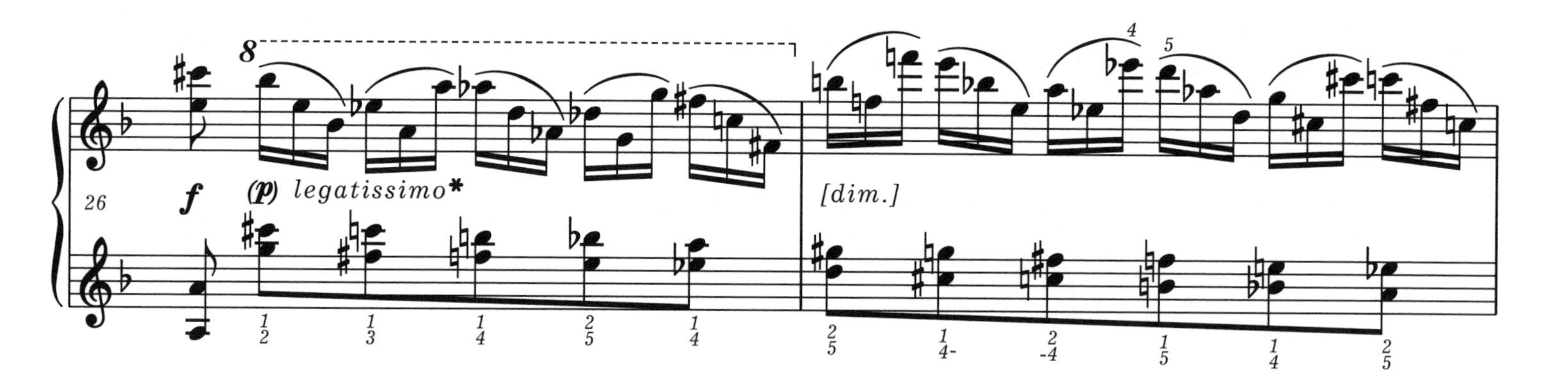

* Patrz *Komentarz wykonawczy.*
Vide *Performance Commentary.*

(TRIO)

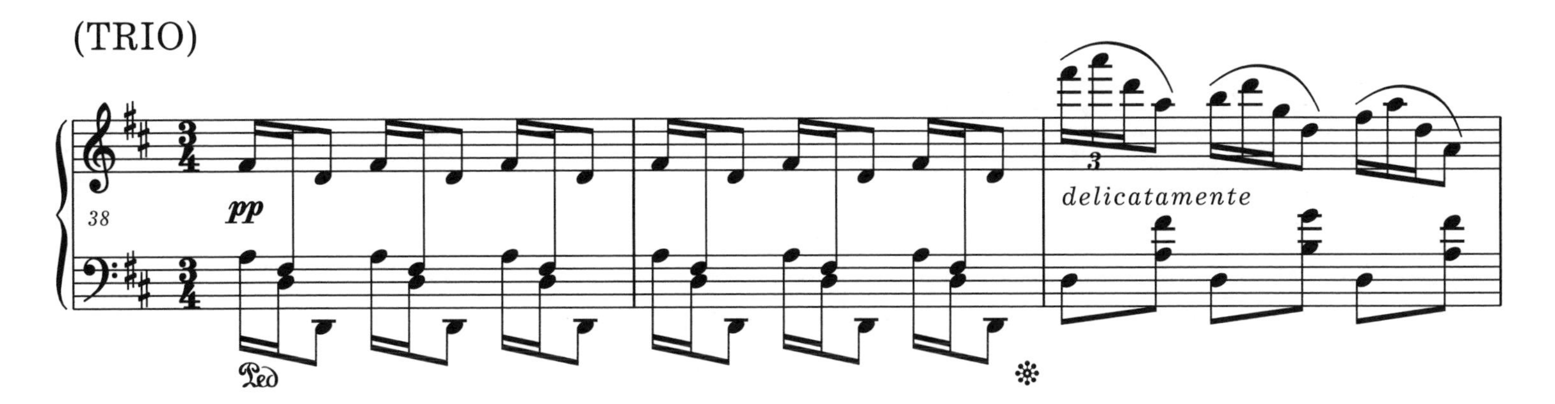

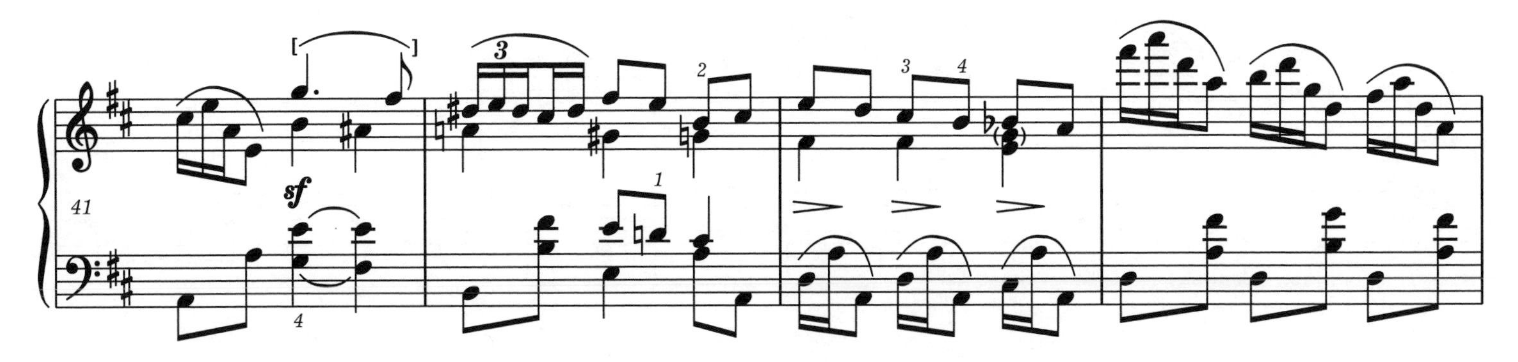

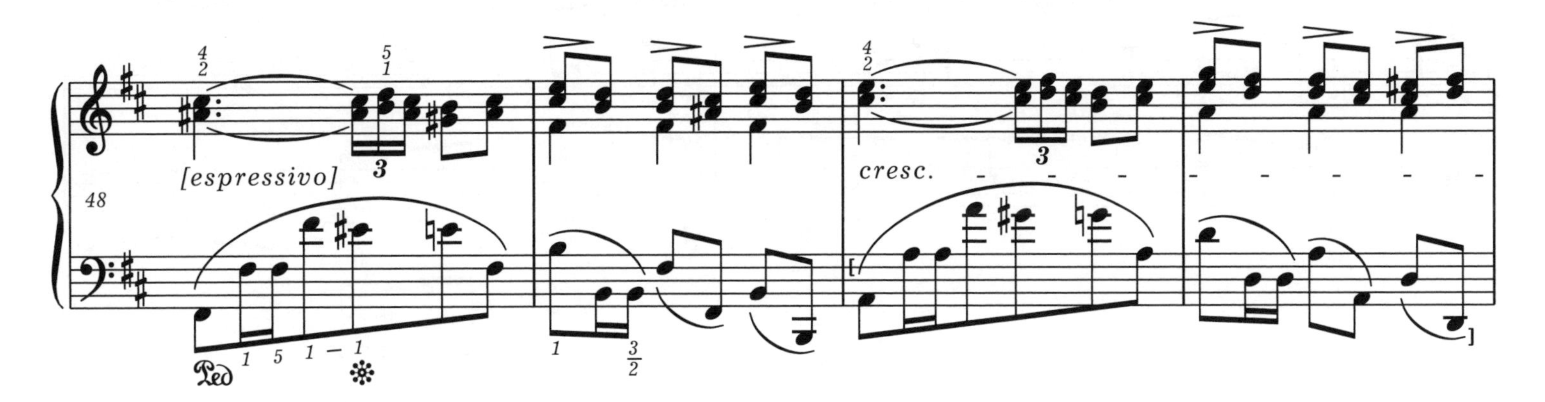

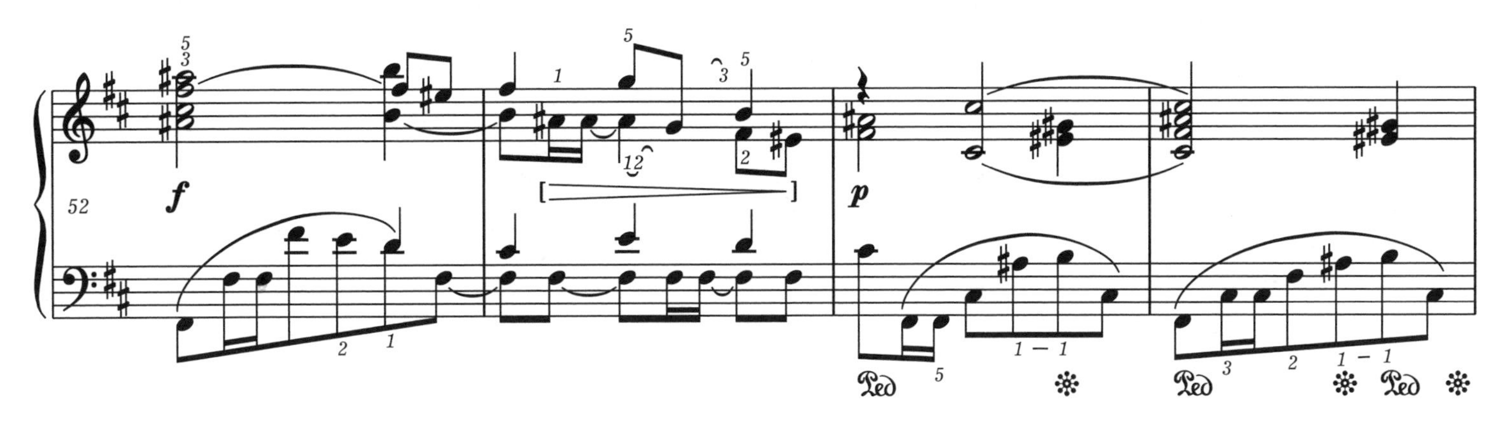

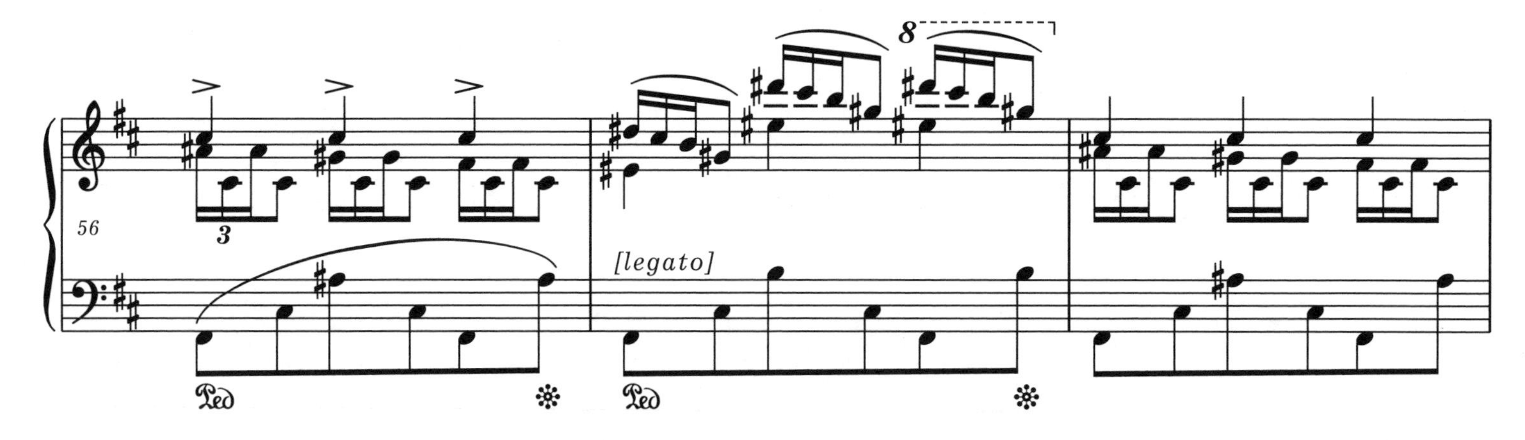

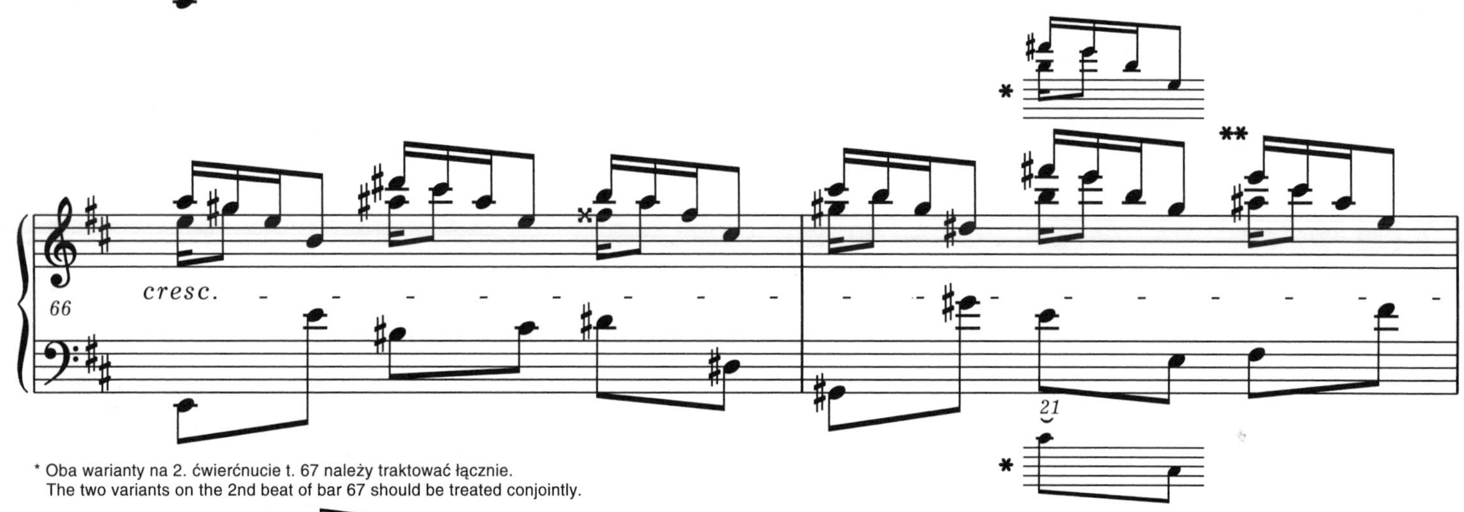

* Oba warianty na 2. ćwierćnucie t. 67 należy traktować łącznie.
The two variants on the 2nd beat of bar 67 should be treated conjointly.

** Dopuszczalny wariant: . Patrz *Komentarz źródłowy.*
Permissible variant: . Vide *Source Commentary.*

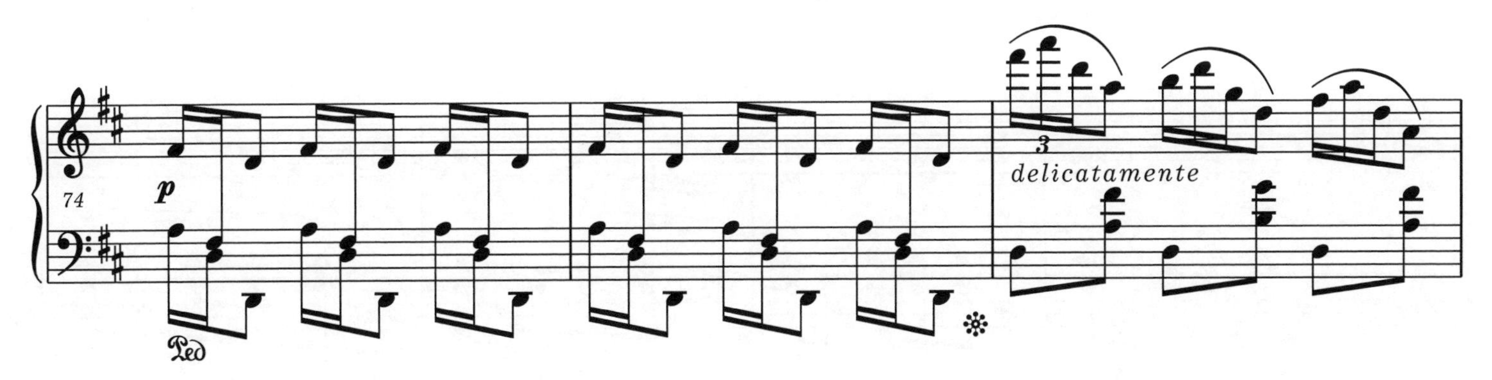

*[Polonaise da Capo al Fine
senza repetizione]*

Polonaise

WN 12

7

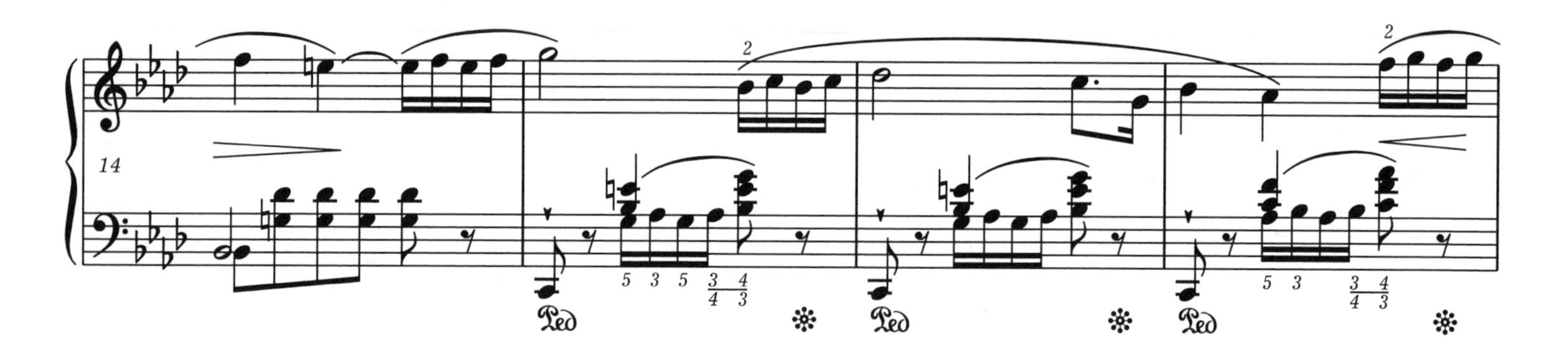

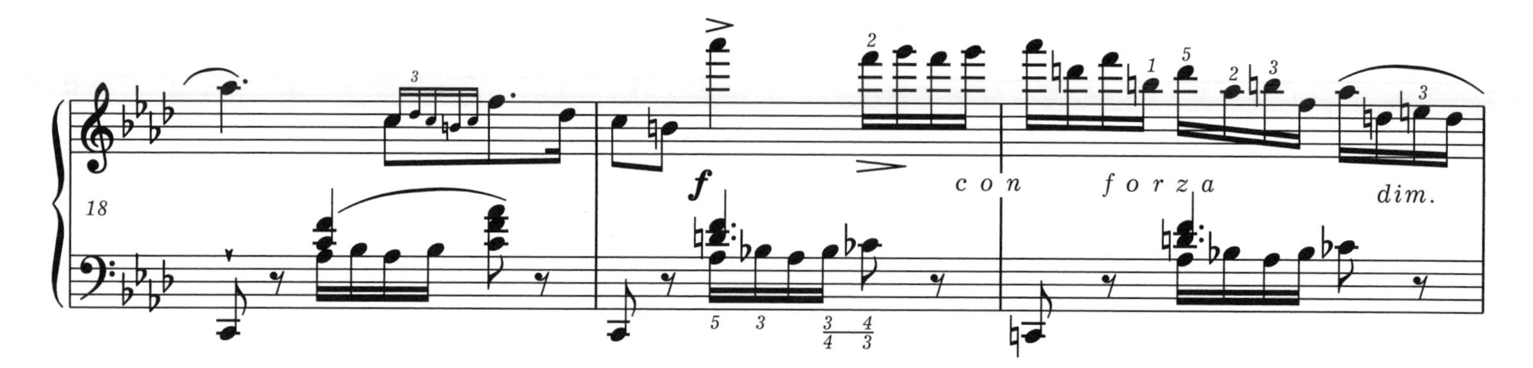

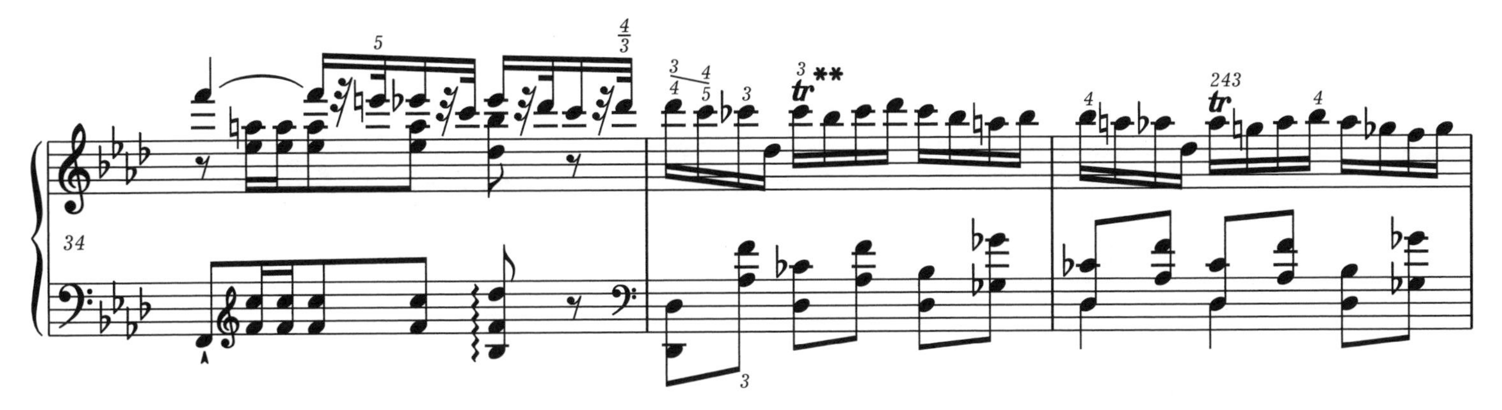

* Dźwięki as^1 w t. 29-30 i des^2 w t. 33-34, notowane w partiach obu rąk, wygodniej wykonać tylko l.r.
The notes ab^1 in bars 29-30 and db^2 in bars 33-34, notated in the parts of both hands, are more comfortably played with the L.H. only.

** **tr** nad szesnastką = ∿ (t. 35-41).
tr above a semiquaver = ∿ (bars 35-41).

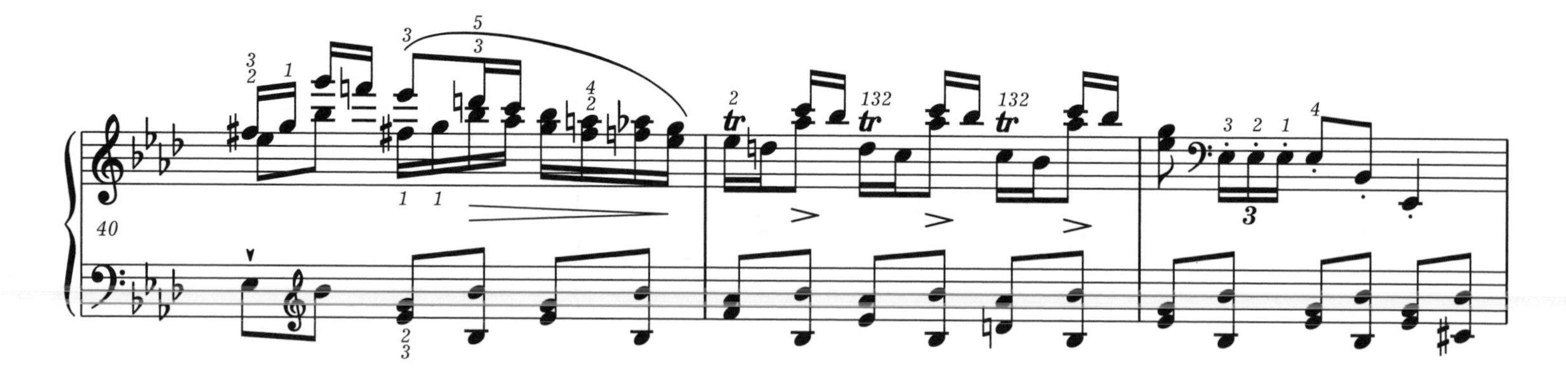

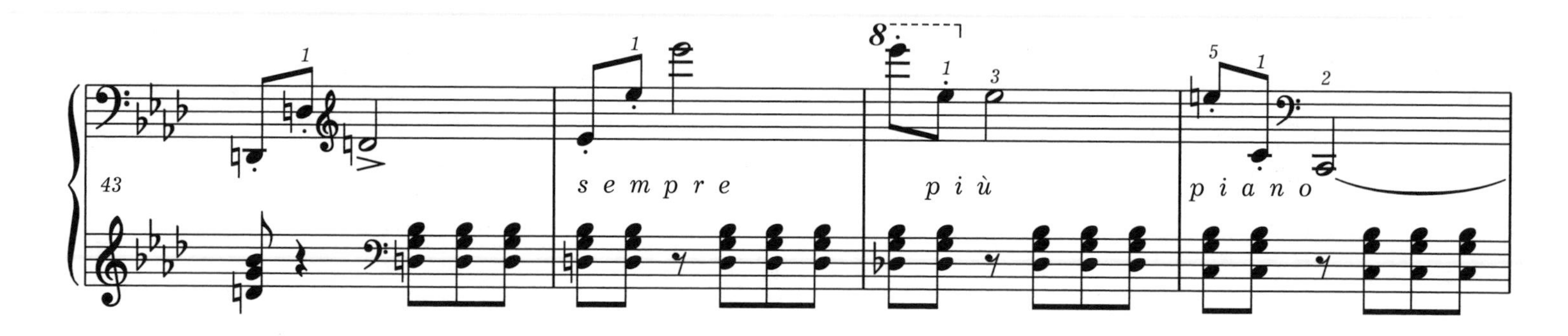

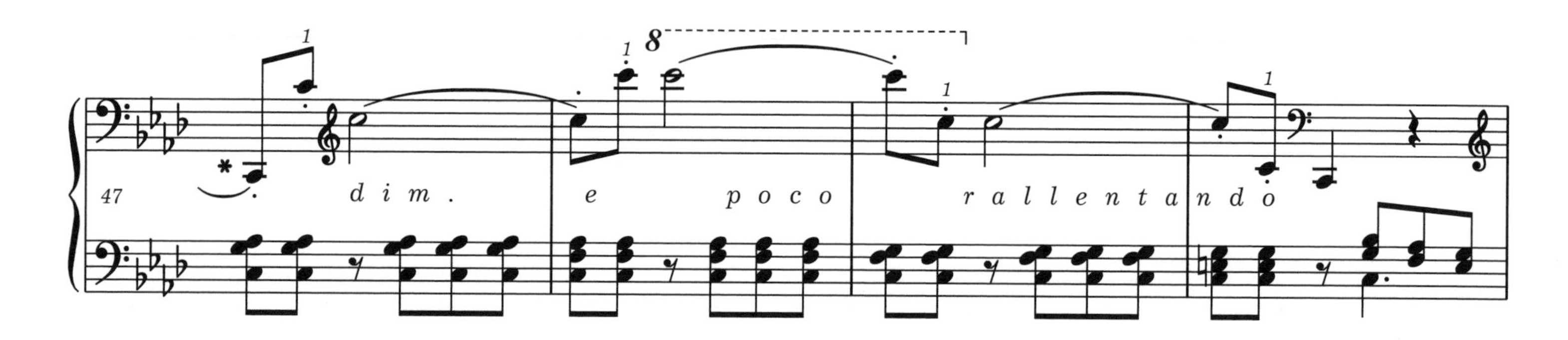

* Kropki *staccato* w t. 47-50 sugerują uderzanie pierwszych ósemek. Patrz *Komentarz źródłowy*.
The *staccato* dots in bars 47-50 suggest the striking of the first quavers. Vide *Source Commentary*.

poco stretto
55

con forza
59

62

con forza
dim.
66
p
pp

mezza voce
69

[Fine]

TRIO

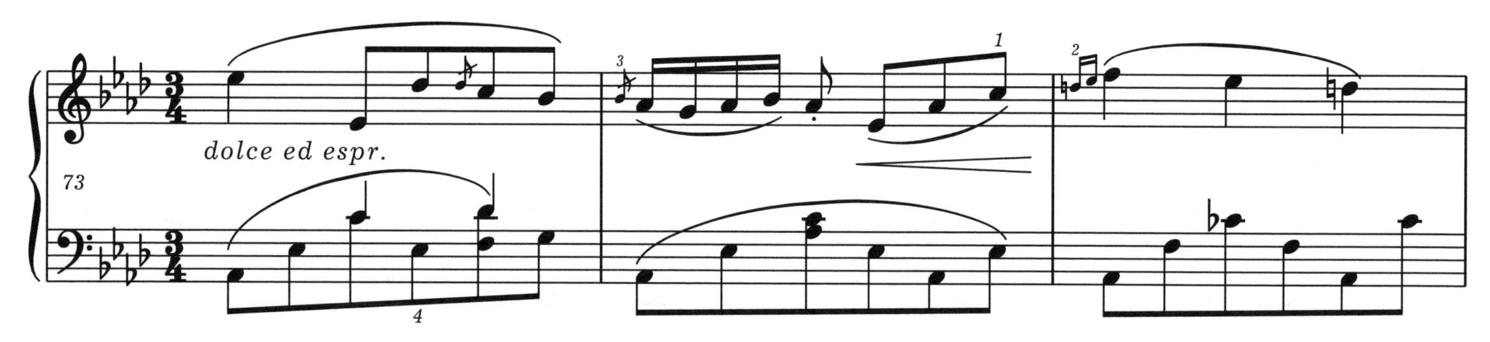

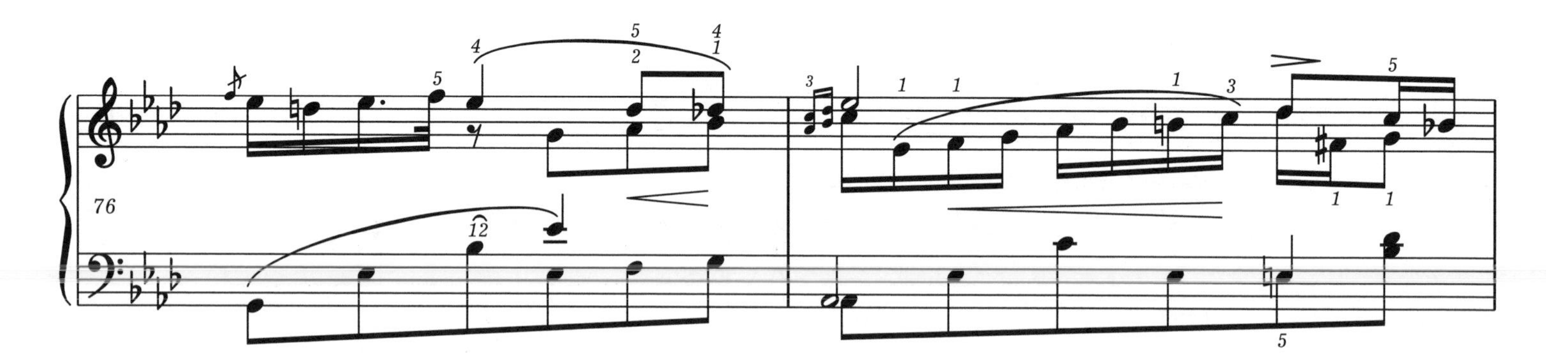

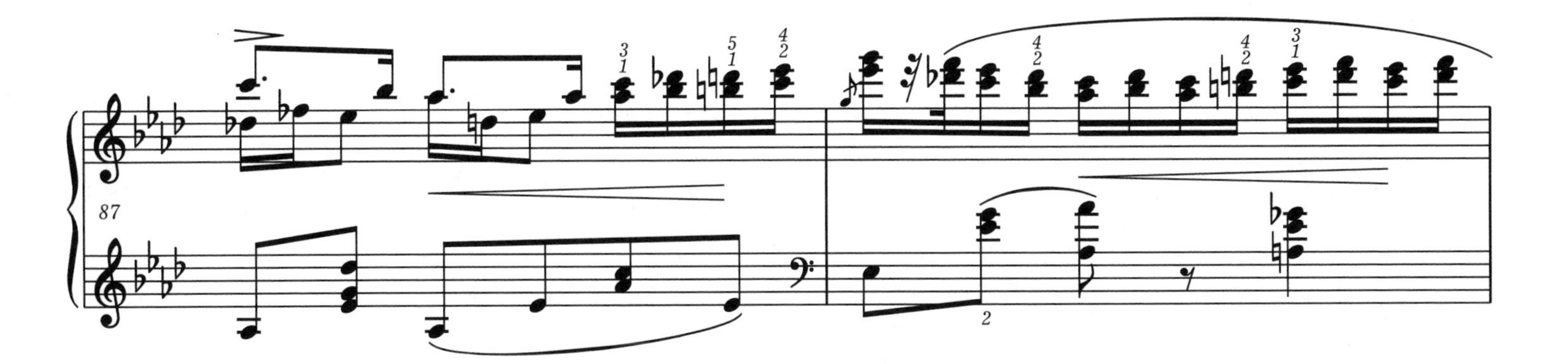

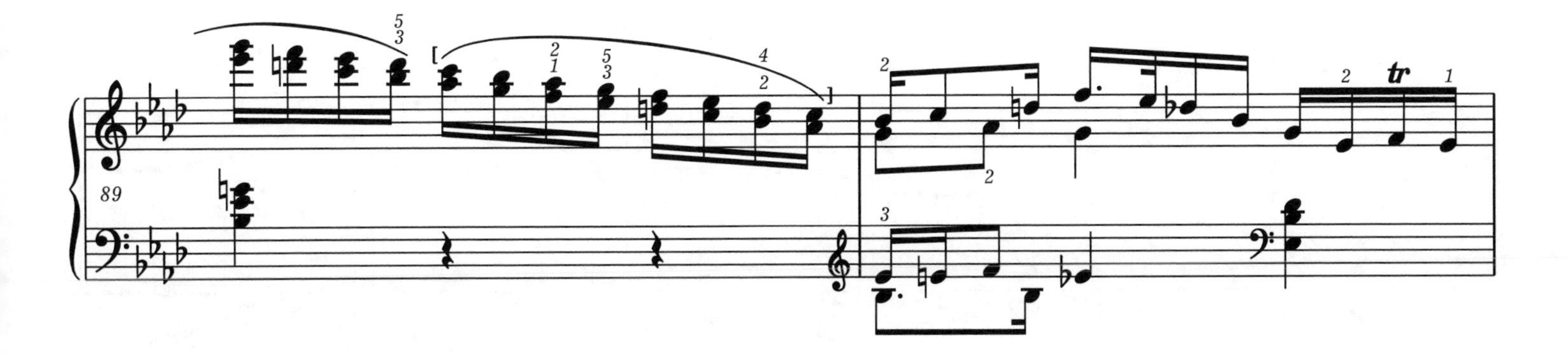

Da Capo al Fine
[senza repetizione]

Polonaise

A M.r A. Ritterich [?]

WN 17

8

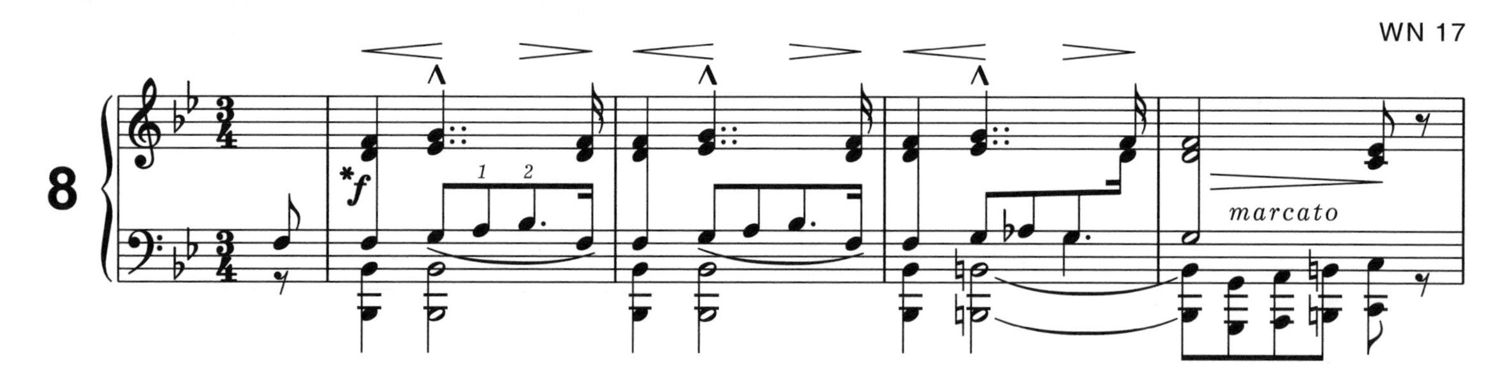

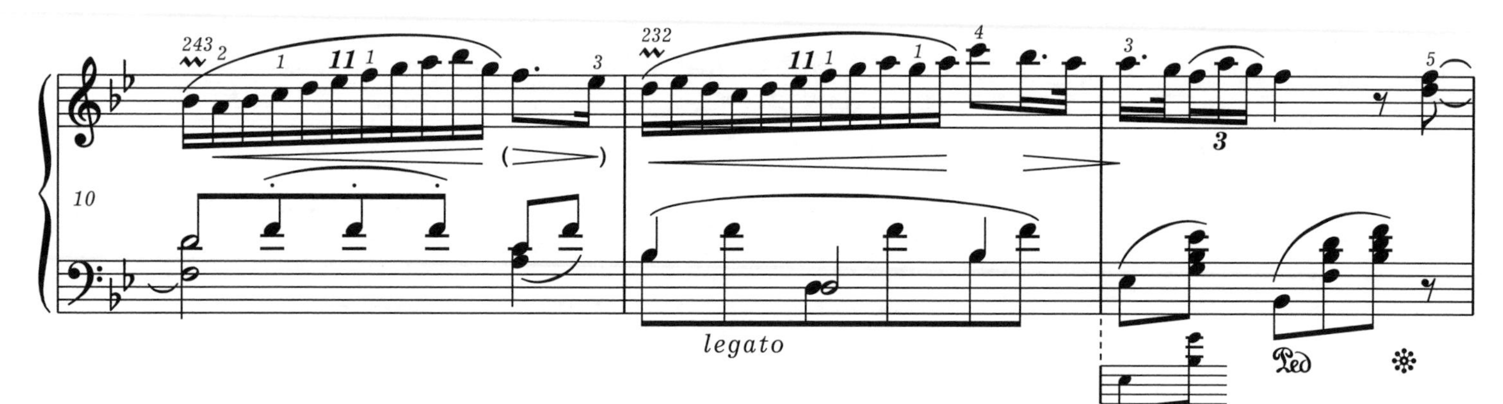

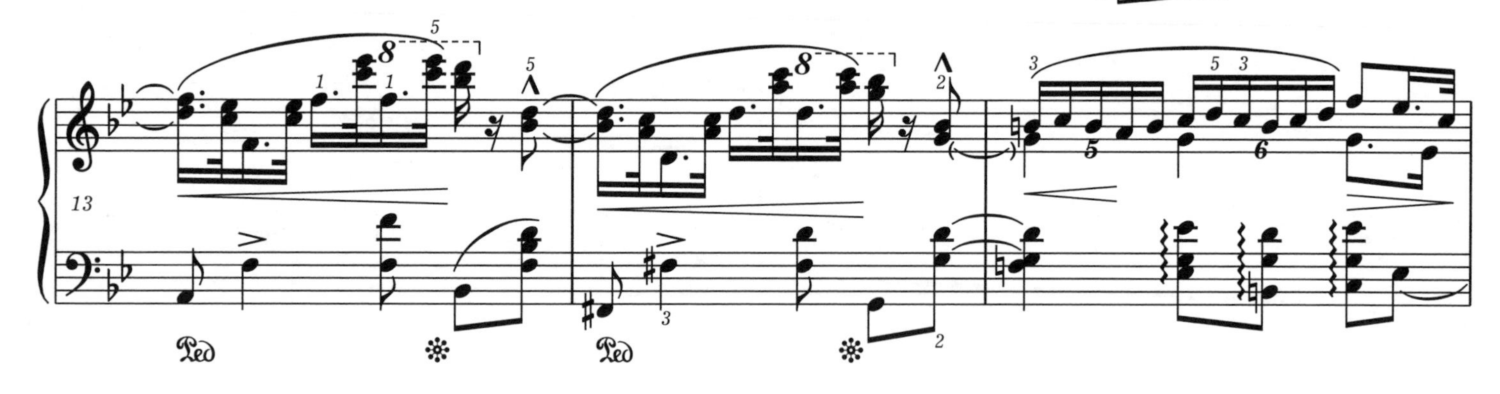

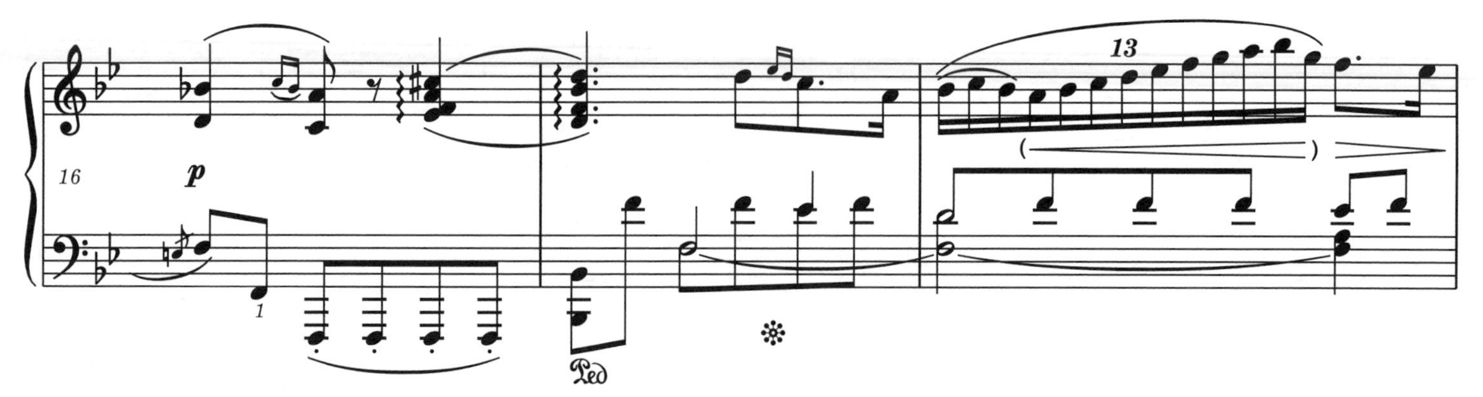

* W jednym ze źródeł ***p***. Patrz *Komentarz źródłowy*.
In one of the sources ***p***. Vide *Source Commentary*.

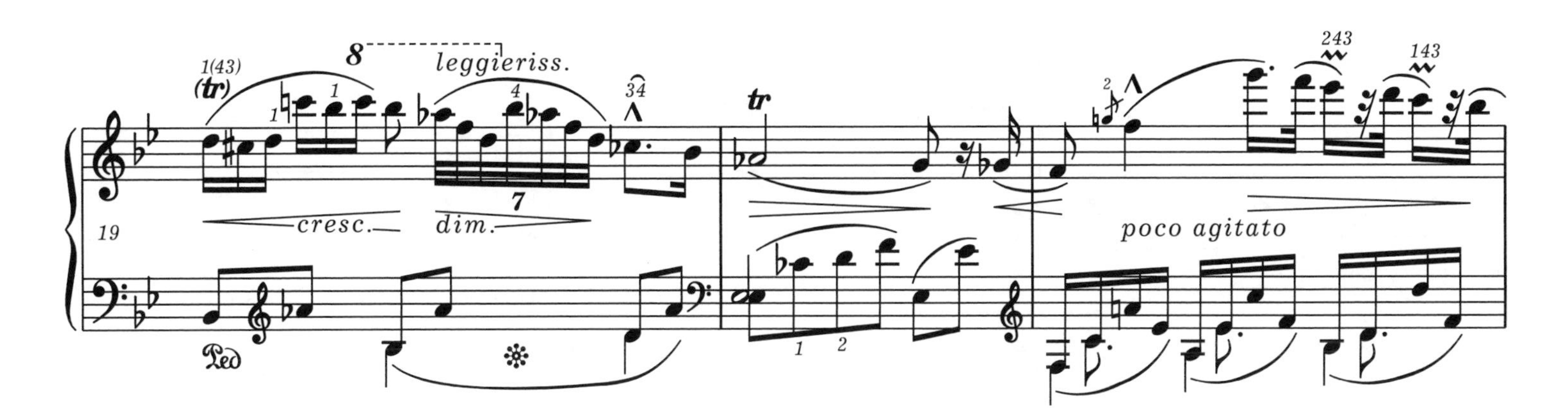

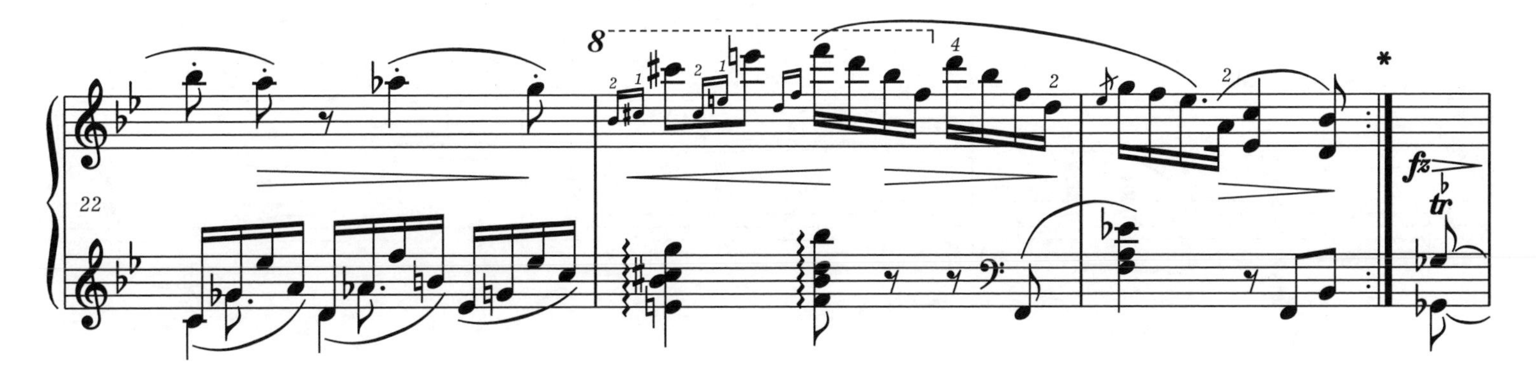

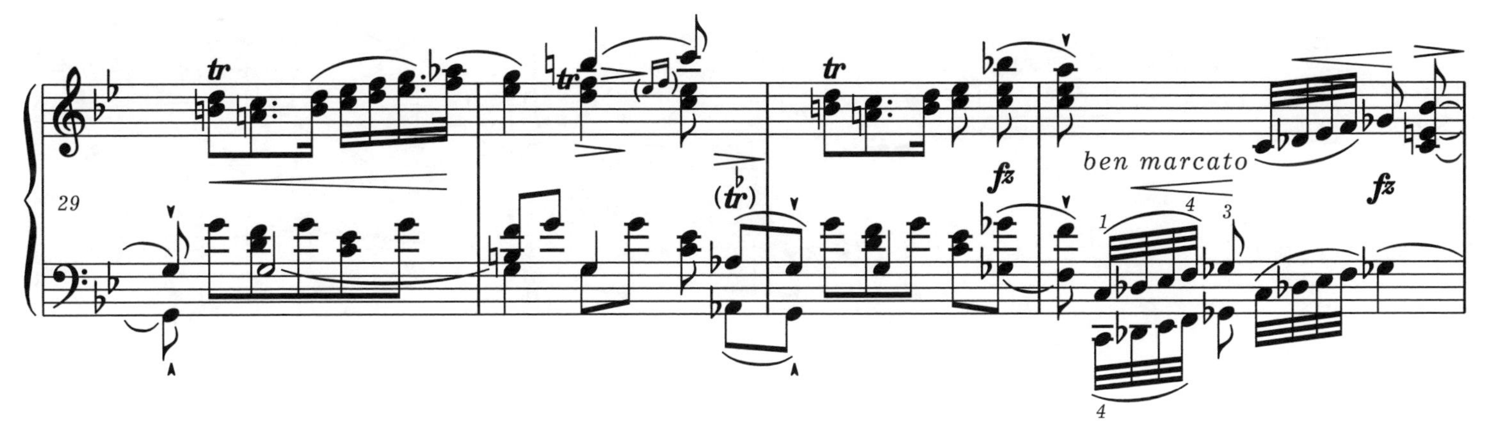

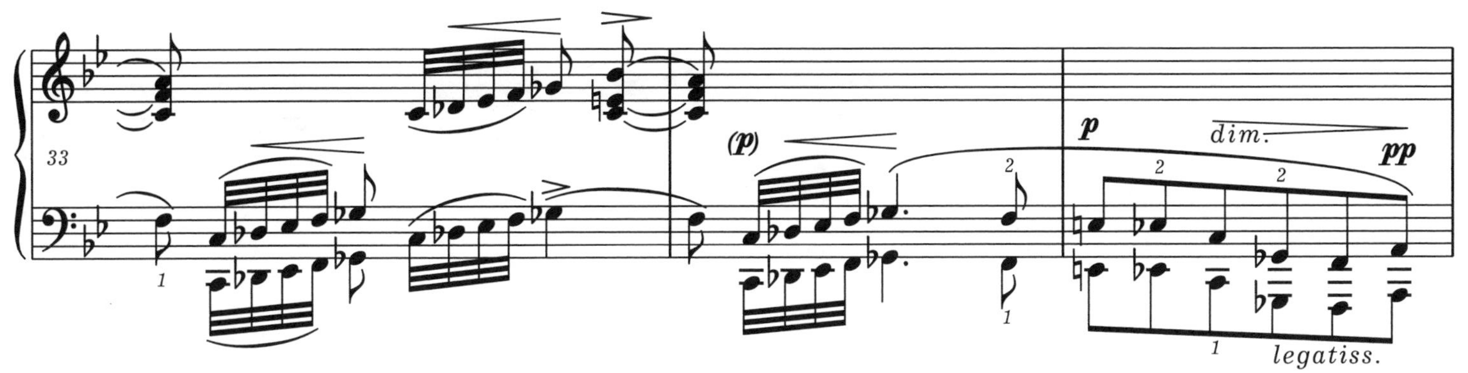

* Patrz *Komentarz wykonawczy* i *źródłowy.*
Vide *Performance* and *Source Commentaries.*

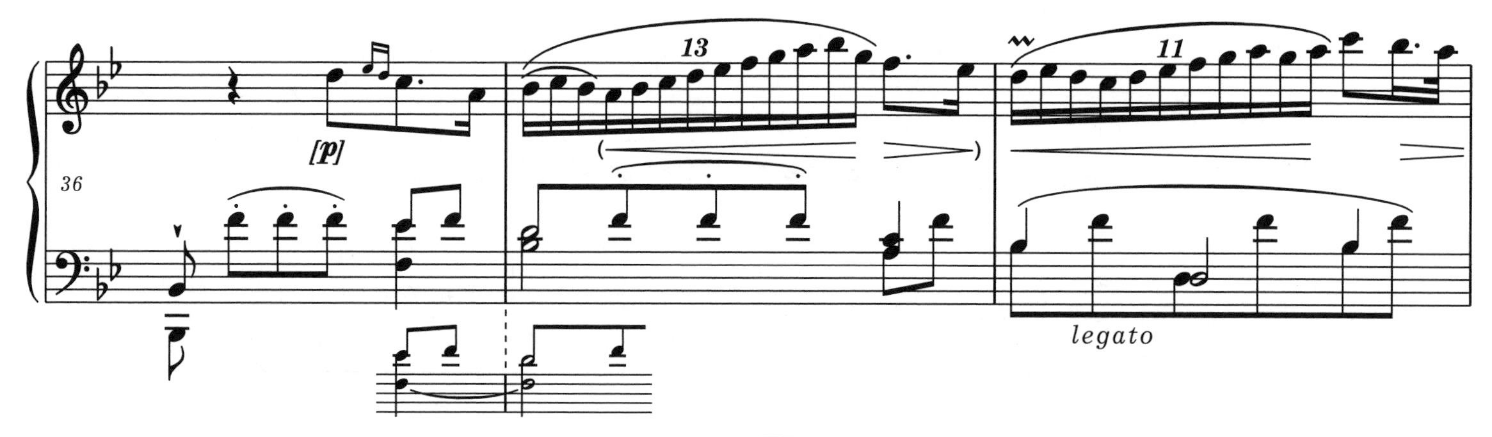

36
[p]
13
11
legato

39
3
8

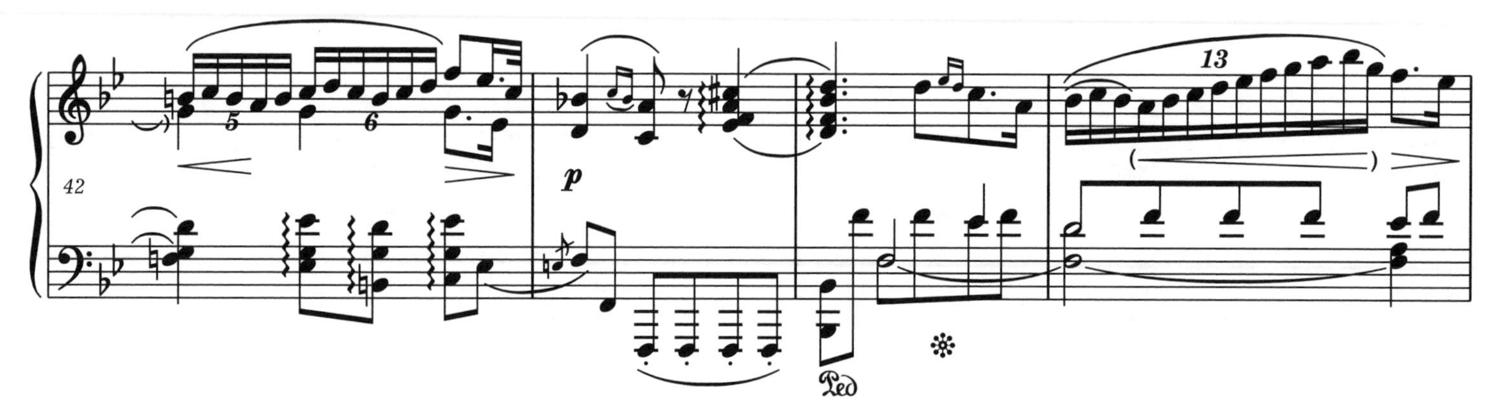

42
5
6
p
13

46
(tr)
8
leggieriss.
cresc.
dim.
7
tr
poco agitato

49
8
[Fine]

TRIO

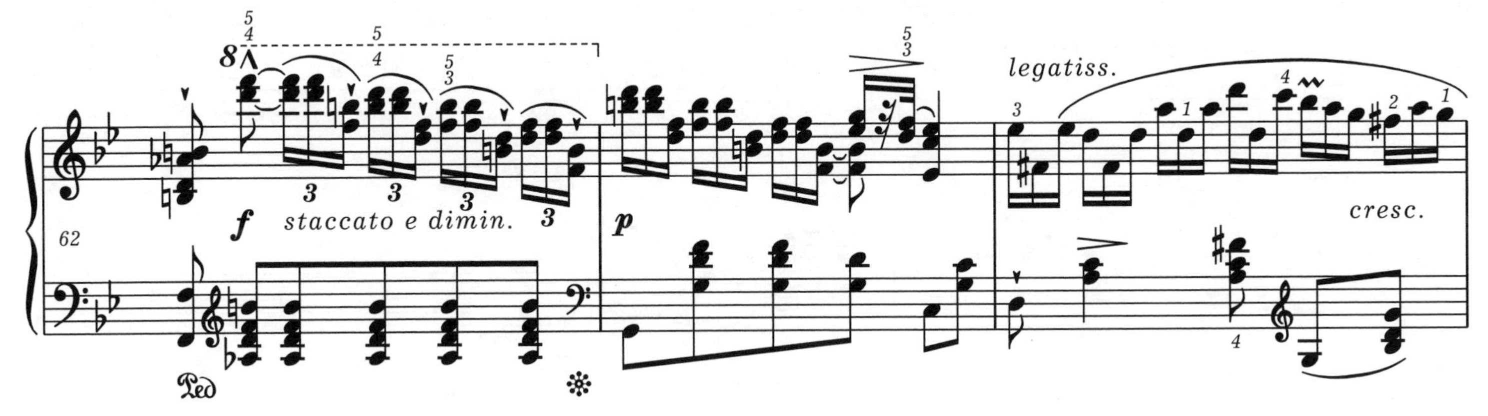

* **tr** = ⁓

** Autentyczność palcowania Chopinowskiego w tym *Polonezie* nie jest pewna. Patrz *Komentarz źródłowy*.
The authenticity of Chopin's fingering in this *Polonaise* is not certain. Vide *Source Commentary*.

sotto voce
pp
ppp
ffz
molto con forza
poco a poco di - mi - nu - en - do
p
pp
ben attaccar
ff
poco
a poco diminuendo
poco rallent.
a tempo
leggiero
p
pp
sempre piano
poco a poco cre - - -
piano ma ben marcato il canto

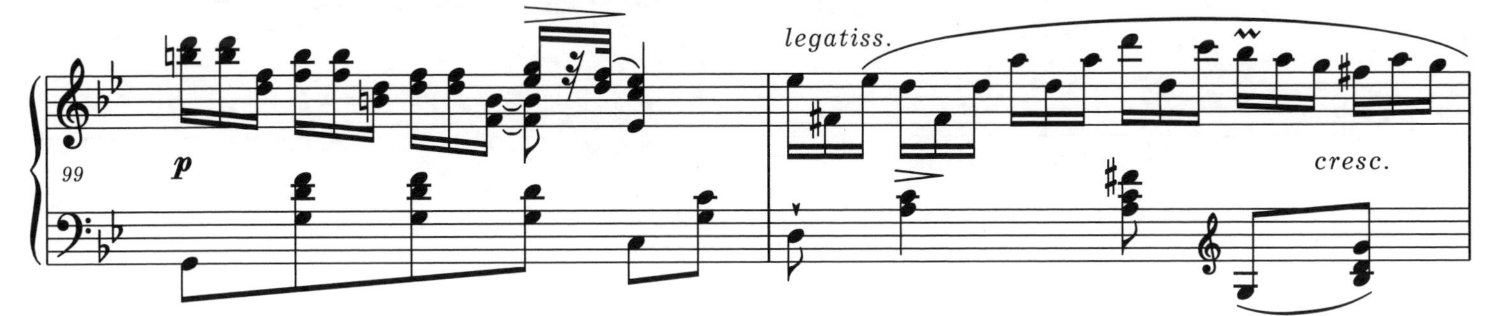

[Da Capo al Fine
senza repetizione]

Polonez

WN 35

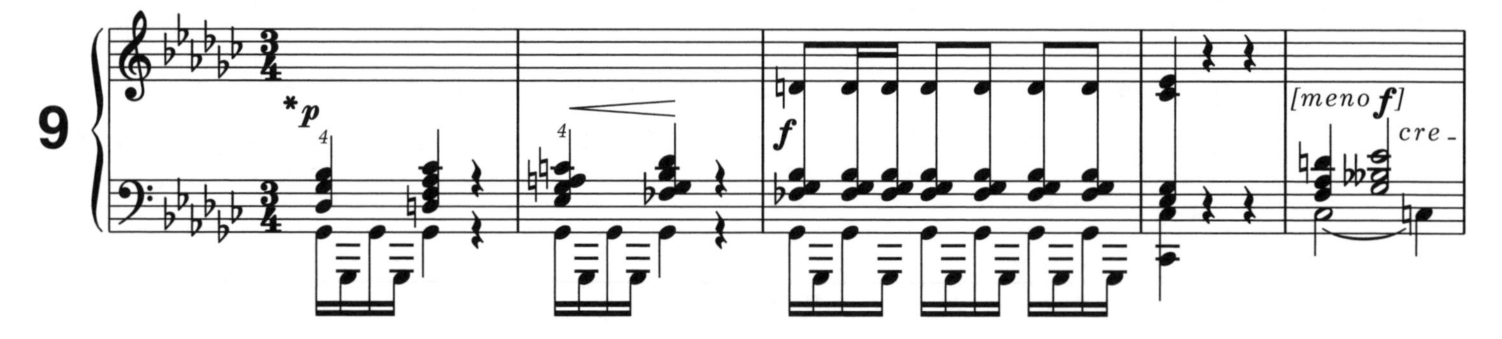

* Autentyczność wszelkich oznaczeń wykonawczych nie jest pewna. Patrz *Komentarz wykonawczy.*
There is uncertainty as to the authenticity of all performance markings. Vide *Performance Commentary.*

** Pedalizacja pochodzi w całości od redakcji.
The pedalling is given entirely by the editors.

*** Tekst zakończenia t. 16 i 46 jest niepewny. Wariant l.r. zalecany przez redakcję: . Patrz *Komentarz źródłowy.*
The text at the end of bars 16 & 46 is uncertain. Variant of the L.H. recommended by the editors: . Vide *Source Commentary.*

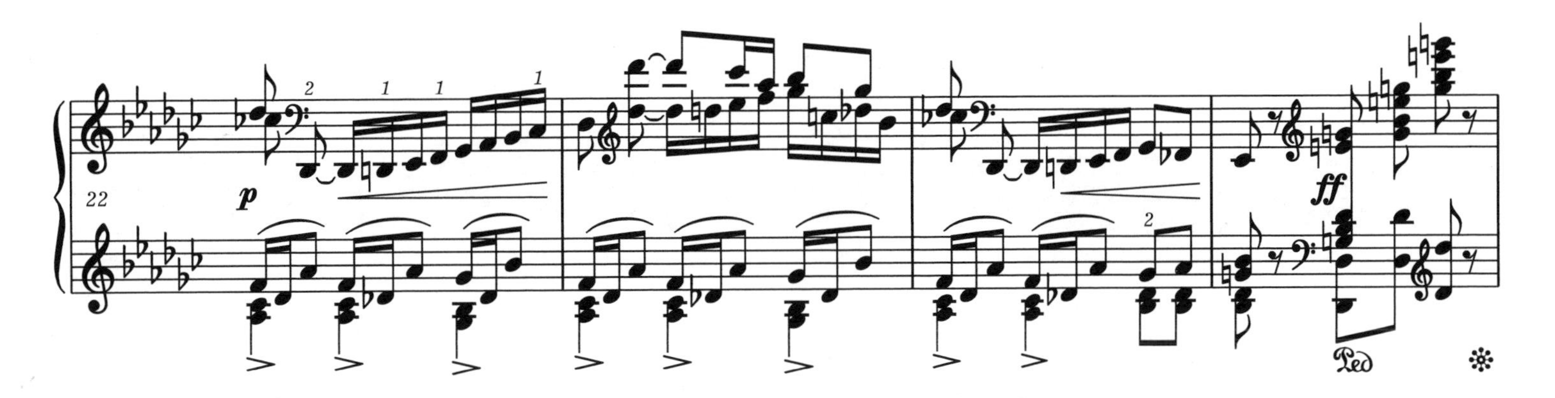
22
p
ff
Ped

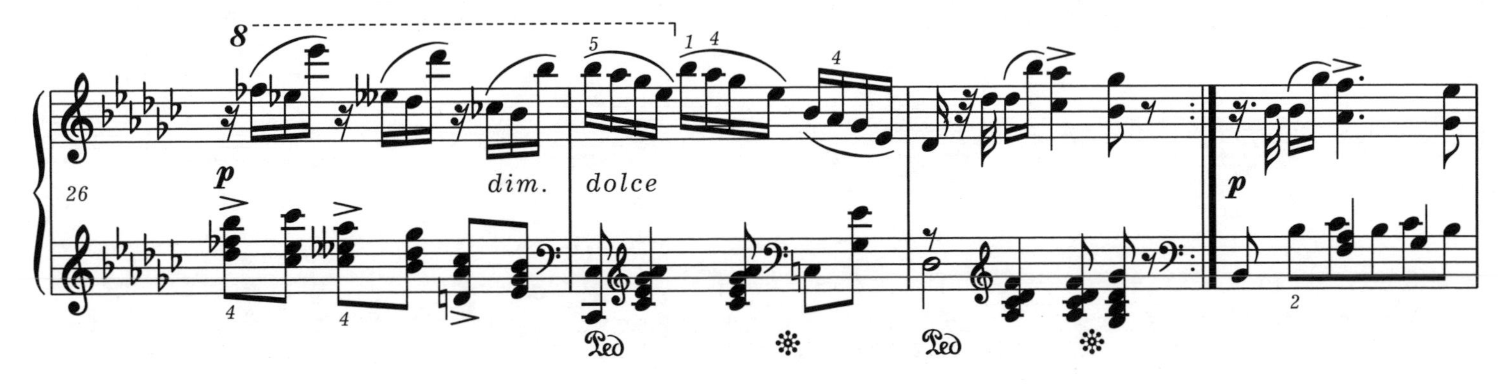
8
26
p
dim.
dolce
Ped
Ped

30

8
33
una corda
pp
Ped
Ped
tre corde
f
Ped

8
36
di - mi - nu - en - do
Ped
Ped

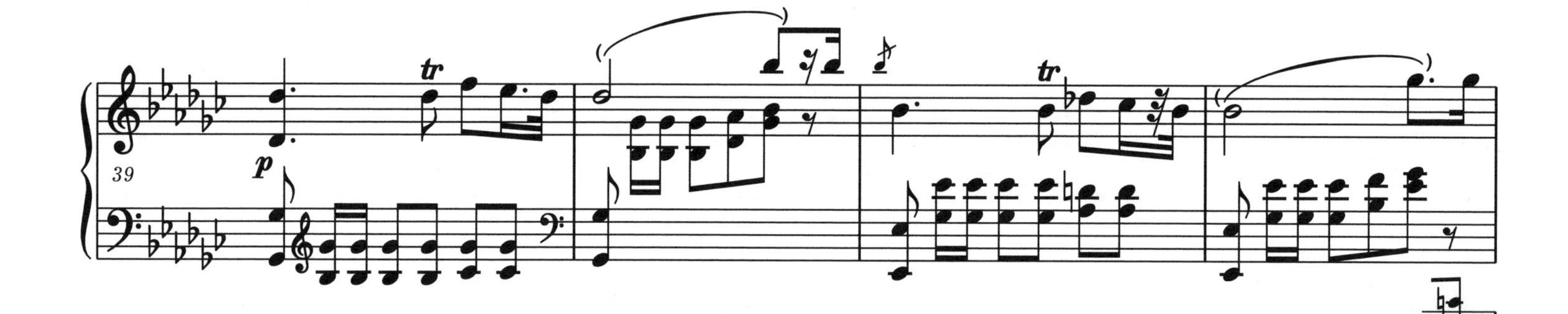

* Patrz uwaga do t. 16 na s. 46.
Vide note to bar 16 on page 46.

TRIO

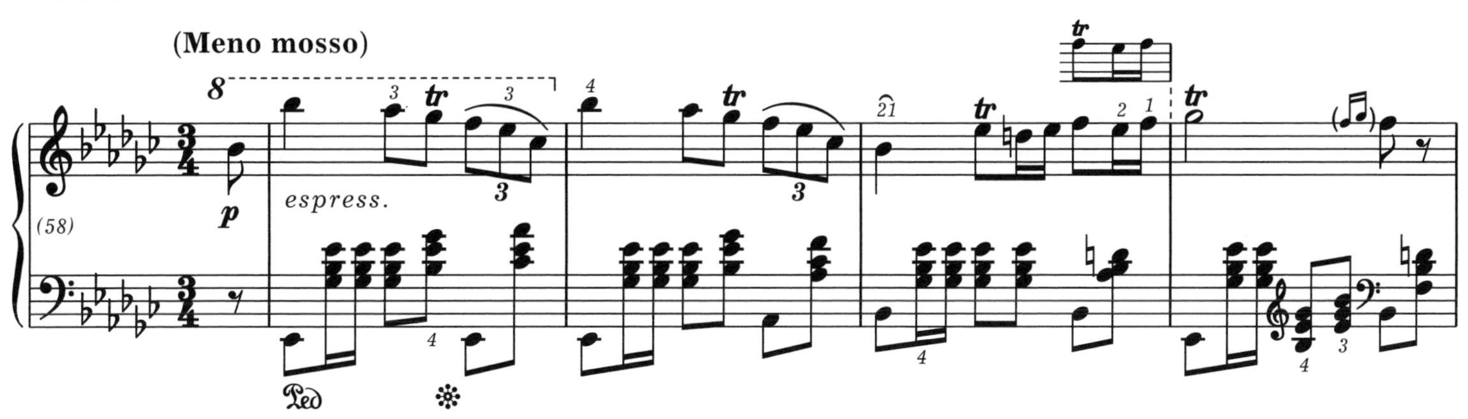
(Meno mosso)
8
tr
espress.
p
(58)

espress.
63
f
8
pp

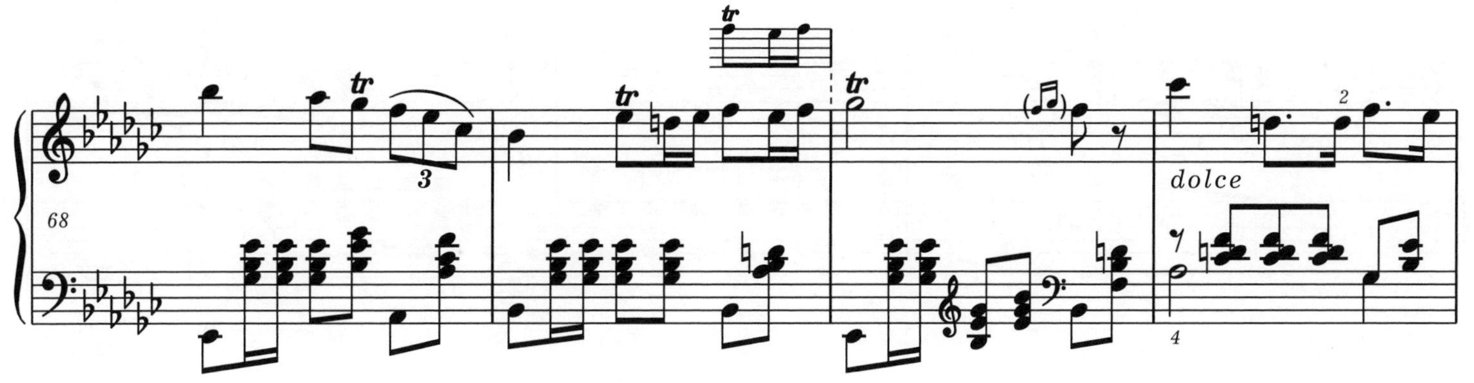
tr
68
dolce

72
f
ten.

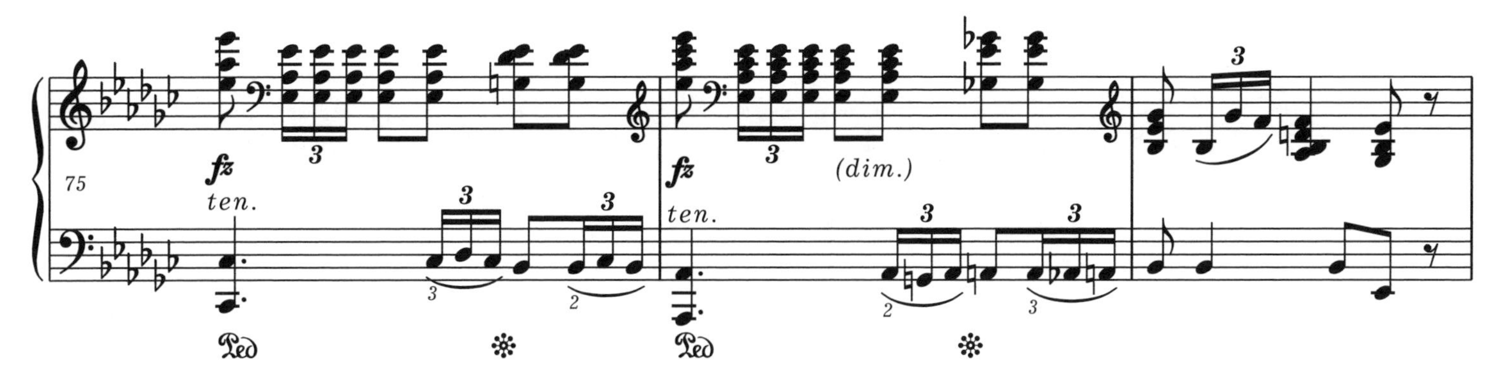
fz
ten.
75
(dim.)

78
p dolce

81
pp
p

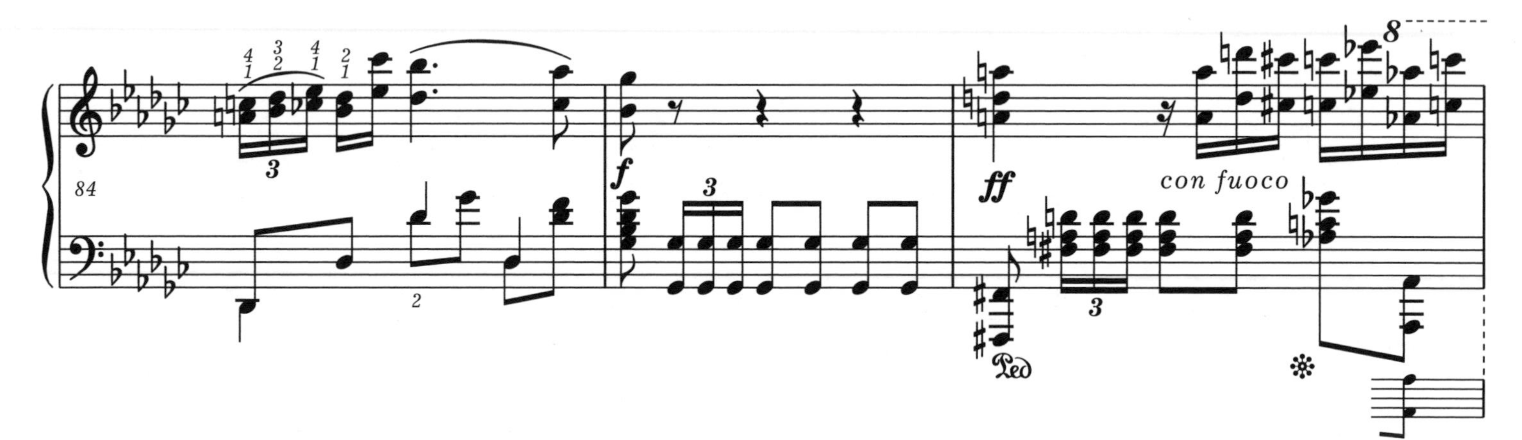
84
f
ff
con fuoco

87

90
p

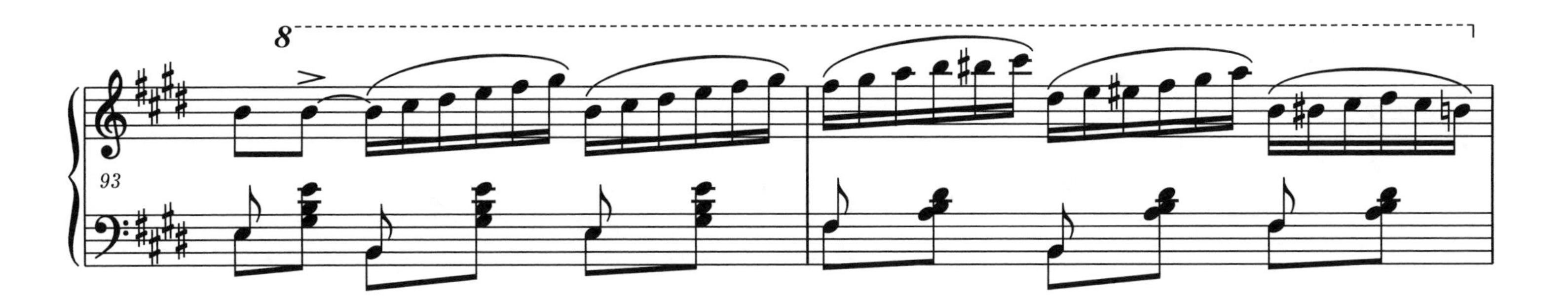
8
93

8
95
p dolce

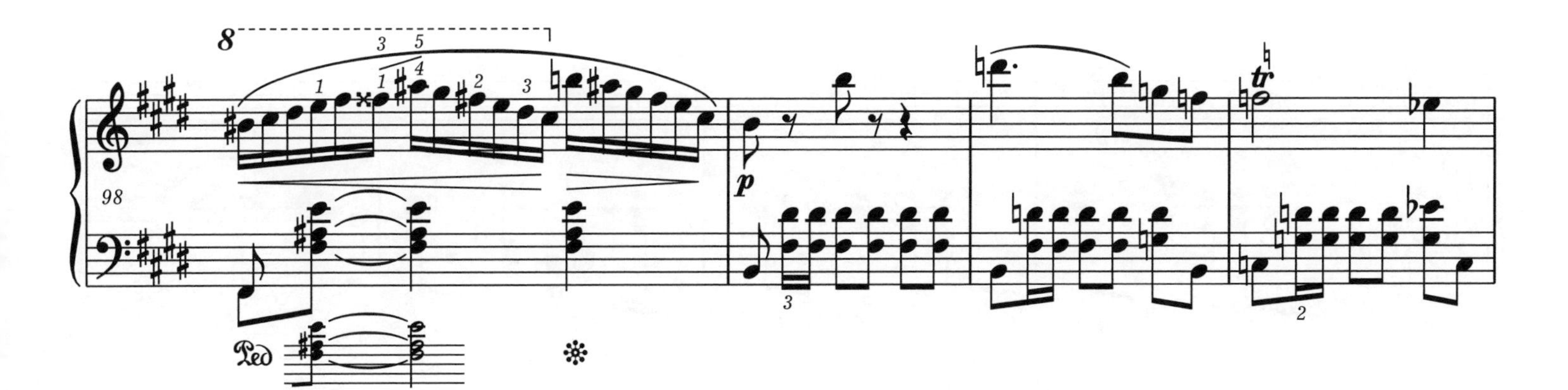
8
98
p
Ped

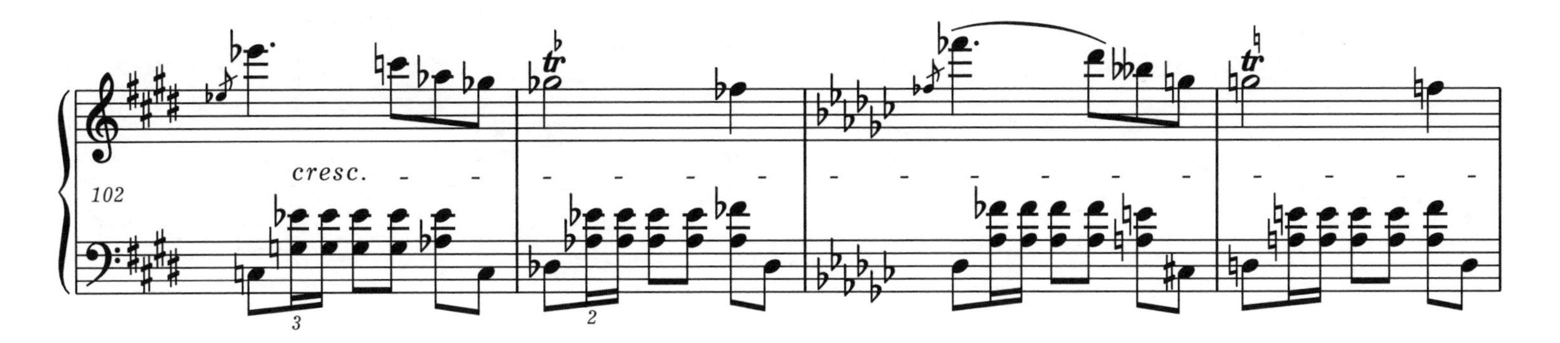
102
cresc.

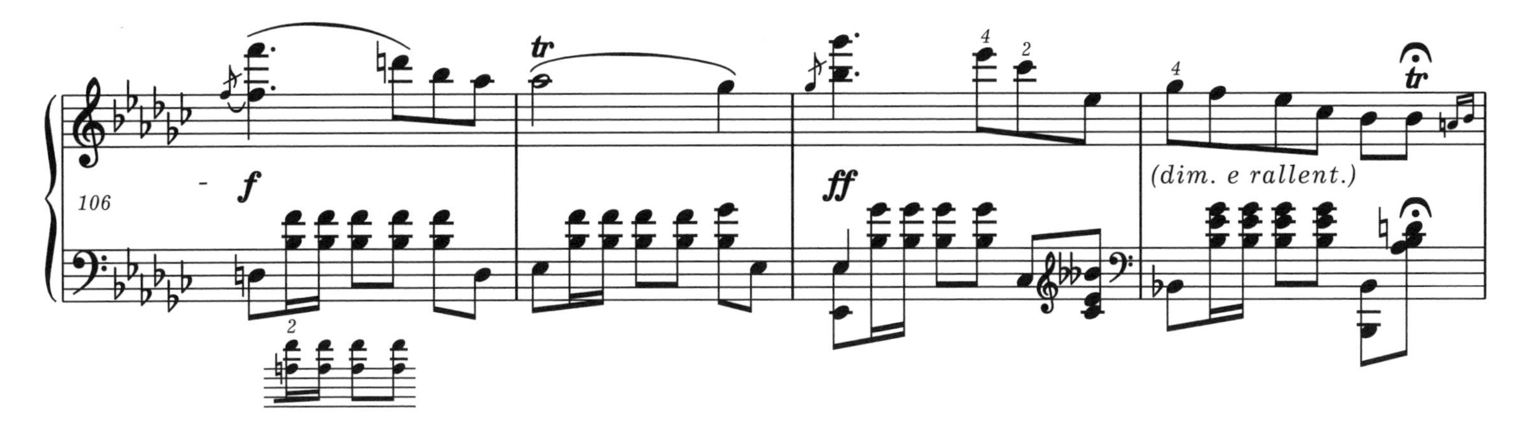
106
f
ff
(dim. e rallent.)

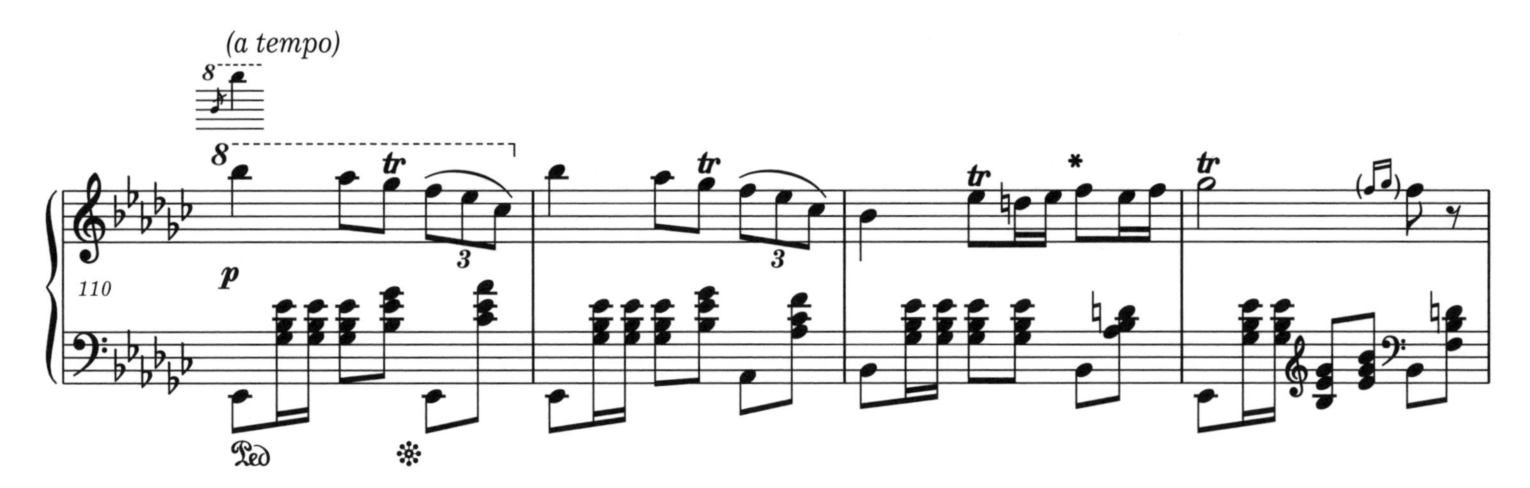

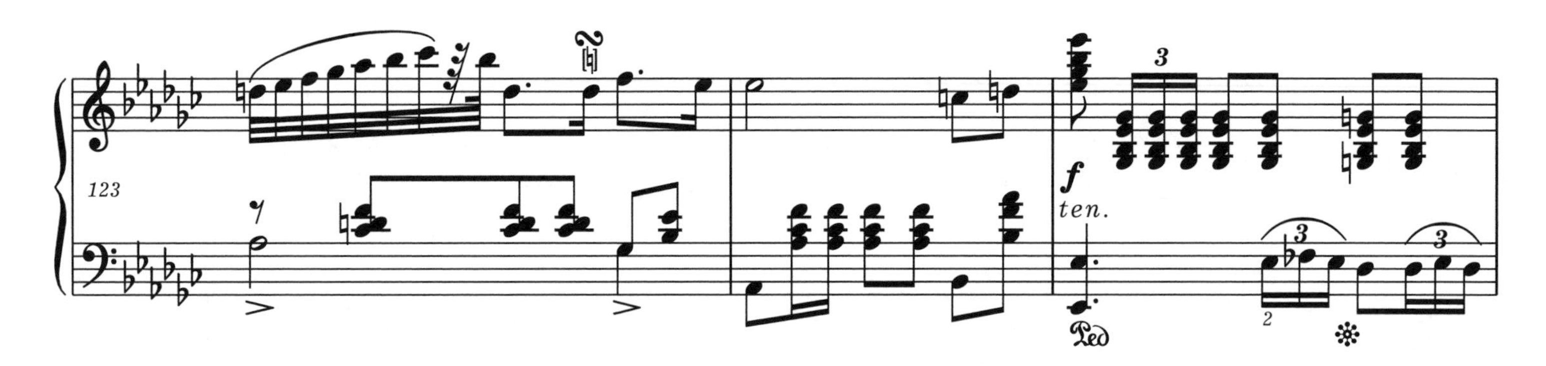

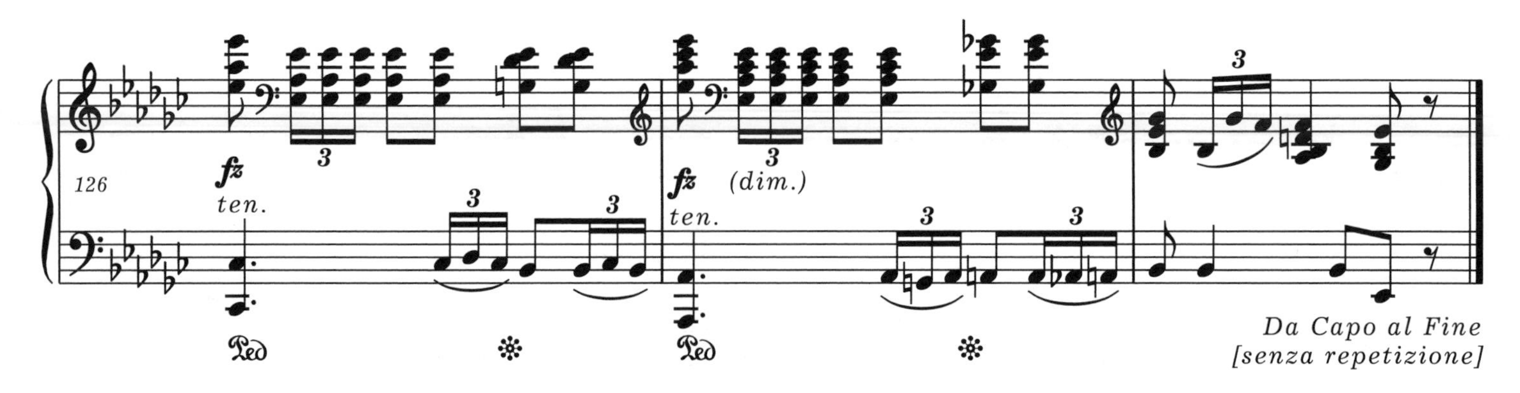

* Warianty jak w t. 61 i 69.
Variants as in bars 61 & 69.

DODATEK • APPENDIX

Polonaise

A Monsieur A. Żywny

Wcześniejsza wersja / Earlier version

* Patrz uwaga na s. 17.
Vide note on page 17.

[Fine]

* Patrz uwaga na s. 17.
Vide note on page 17.

TRIO

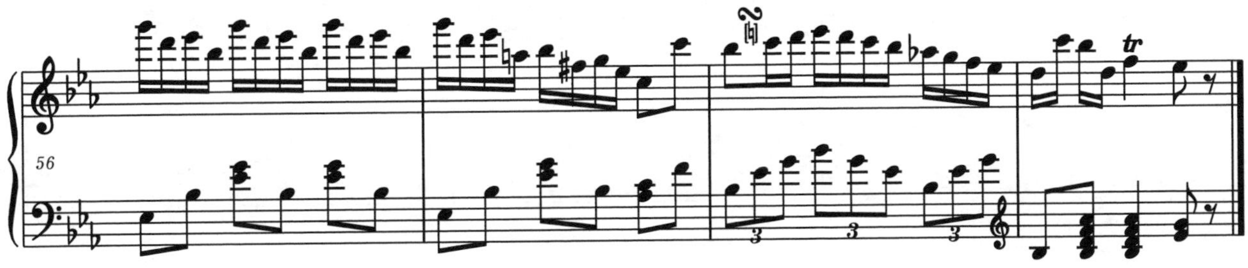

[Polonaise da Capo al Fine
senza repetizione]

Polonaise

Wcześniejsza wersja / Earlier version

WN 12

(7)

* Wcześniejsza wersja t. 20 i 66:  . Patrz *Komentarz źródłowy*.
Earlier version of bars 20 & 66: . Vide *Source Commentary*.

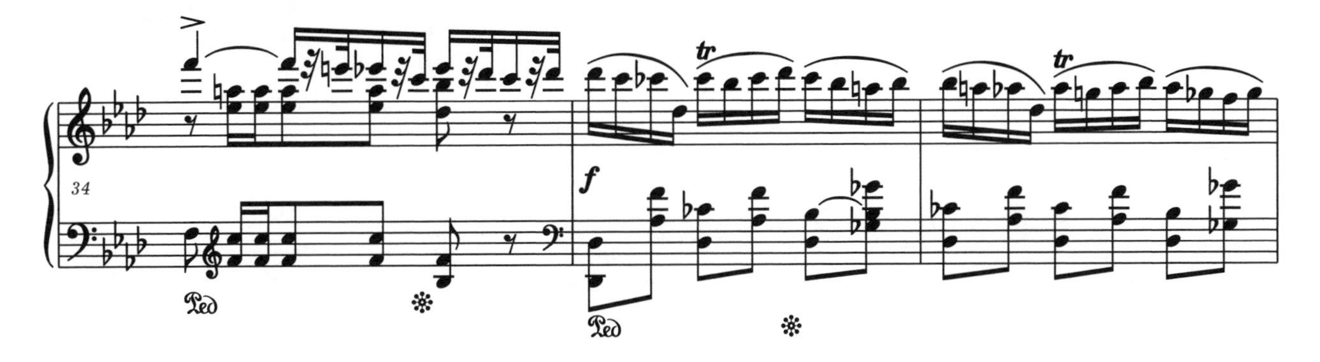

* Autentyczność palcowania Chopinowskiego w tej wersji *Poloneza* nie jest pewna.
The authenticity of Chopin's fingering in this version of the *Polonaise* is not certain.

** W jednym ze źródeł akordy *g-des*^{1}-*e*^{1} w t. 23-24 i 69-70 poprzedzone są znakami arpeggia.
In one of the sources the chords *g-d♭*^{1}-*e*^{1} in bars 23-24 & 69-70 are preceded by arpeggio signs.

37
tr

40
(marcato)
tr

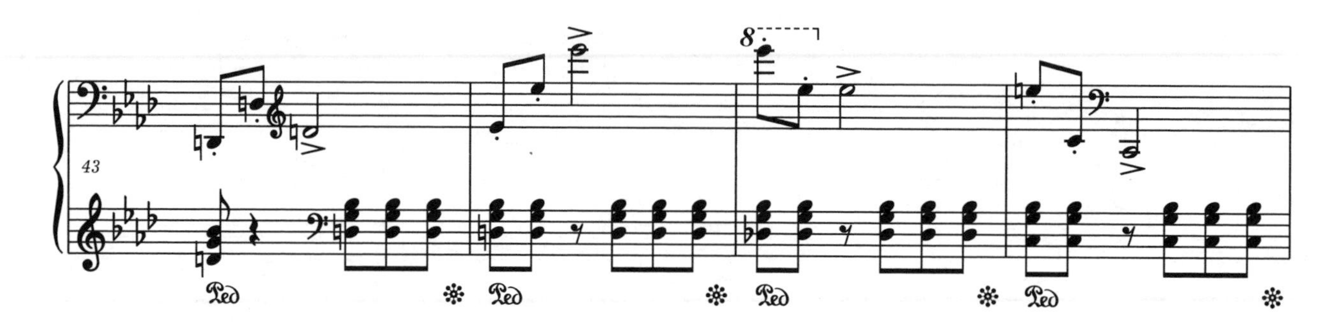
43
Ped

47
p
pp
ppp
Ped

51
(espress.)
ten.
tr

* Wcześniejsza wersja t. 66 – patrz uwaga na s. 58.
For an earlier version of bar 66 vide note on p. 58.

** Patrz uwaga na s. 59.
Vide note on p. 59.

TRIO

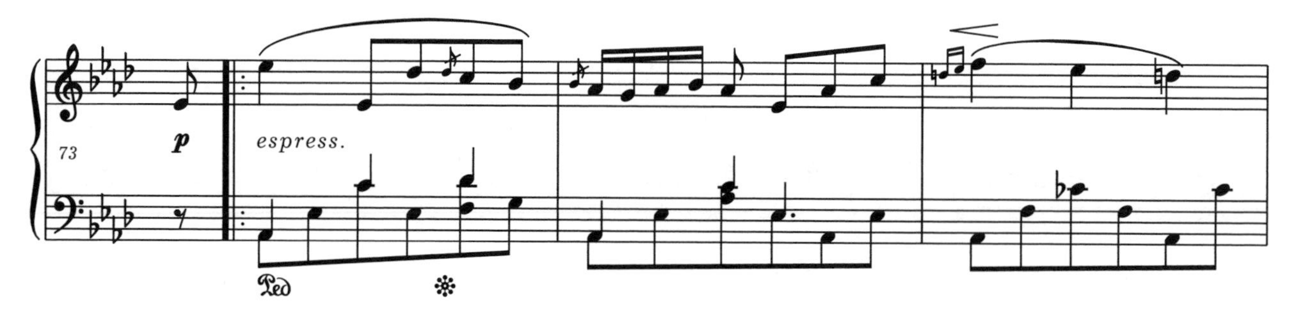

* Wcześniejsza wersja t. 83:
Earlier version of bars 83:

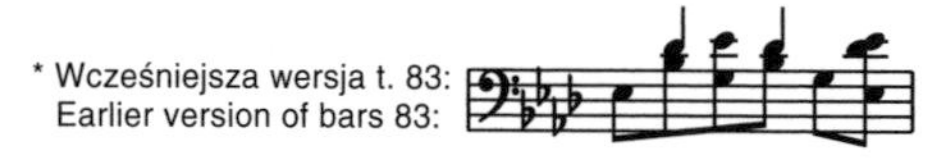

Da Capo al Fine
senza repetizione

WYDANIE NARODOWE DZIEŁ FRYDERYKA CHOPINA

Plan edycji

Seria A. UTWORY WYDANE ZA ŻYCIA CHOPINA

1 **A I** **Ballady** op. 23, 38, 47, 52

2 **A II** **Etiudy** op. 10, 25, Trzy Etiudy (Méthode des Méthodes)

3 **A III** **Impromptus** op. 29, 36, 51

4 **A IV** **Mazurki (A)** op. 6, 7, 17, 24, 30, 33, 41, Mazurek a (Gaillard), Mazurek a (z albumu La France Musicale /Notre Temps/), op. 50, 56, 59, 63

5 **A V** **Nokturny** op. 9, 15, 27, 32, 37, 48, 55, 62

6 **A VI** **Polonezy (A)** op. 26, 40, 44, 53, 61

7 **A VII** **Preludia** op. 28, 45

8 **A VIII** **Ronda** op. 1, 5, 16

9 **A IX** **Scherza** op. 20, 31, 39, 54

10 **A X** **Sonaty** op. 35, 58

11 **A XI** **Walce (A)** op. 18, 34, 42, 64

12 **A XII** **Dzieła różne (A)** Variations brillantes op. 12, Bolero, Tarantela, Allegro de concert, Fantazja op. 49, Berceuse, Barkarola; *suplement* – Wariacja VI z „Hexameronu"

13 **A XIIIa** **Koncert e-moll** op. 11 na fortepian i orkiestrę (wersja na jeden fortepian)

14 **A XIIIb** **Koncert f-moll** op. 21 na fortepian i orkiestrę (wersja na jeden fortepian)

15 **A XIVa** **Utwory koncertowe** na fortepian i orkiestrę op. 2, 13, 14 (wersja na jeden fortepian)

16 **A XIVb** **Polonez Es-dur** op. 22 na fortepian i orkiestrę (wersja na jeden fortepian)

17 **A XVa** **Wariacje na temat z *Don Giovanniego* Mozarta** op. 2. Partytura

18 **A XVb** **Koncert e-moll** op. 11. Partytura (wersja historyczna)

19 **A XVc** **Fantazja na tematy polskie** op. 13. Partytura

20 **A XVd** **Krakowiak** op. 14. Partytura

21 **A XVe** **Koncert f-moll** op. 21. Partytura (wersja historyczna)

22 **A XVf** **Polonez Es-dur** op. 22. Partytura

23 **A XVI** **Utwory na fortepian i wiolonczelę** Polonez op. 3, Grand Duo Concertant, Sonata op. 65

24 **A XVII** **Trio na fortepian, skrzypce i wiolonczelę** op. 8

Seria B. UTWORY WYDANE POŚMIERTNIE

(Tytuły w nawiasach kwadratowych [] są tytułami zrekonstruowanymi przez WN, tytuły w nawiasach prostych // są dotychczas używanymi, z pewnością lub dużym prawdopodobieństwem, nieautentycznymi tytułami)

25 **B I** **Mazurki (B)** B, G, a, C, F, G, B, As, C, a, g, f

26 **B II** **Polonezy (B)** B, g, As, gis, d, f, b, B, Ges

27 **B III** **Walce (B)** E, h, Des, As, e, Ges, As, f, a

28 **B IV** **Dzieła różne (B)** Wariacje E, Sonata c (op. 4)

29 **B V** **Różne utwory** Marsz żałobny c, [Warianty] /Souvenir de Paganini/, Nokturn e, Ecossaises D, G, Des, Kontredans, [Allegretto], Lento con gran espressione /Nokturn cis/, Cantabile B, Presto con leggierezza /Preludium As/, Impromptu cis /Fantaisie-Impromptu/, „Wiosna" (wersja na fortepian), Sostenuto /Walc Es/, Moderato /Kartka z albumu/, Galop Marquis, Nokturn c

30 **B VIa** **Koncert e-moll** op. 11 na fortepian i orkiestrę (wersja z drugim fortepianem)

31 **B VIb** **Koncert f-moll** op. 21 na fortepian i orkiestrę (wersja z drugim fortepianem)

32 **B VII** **Utwory koncertowe** na fortepian i orkiestrę op. 2, 13, 14, 22 (wersja z drugim fortepianem)

33 **B VIIIa** **Koncert e-moll** op. 11. Partytura (wersja koncertowa)

34 **B VIIIb** **Koncert f-moll** op. 21. Partytura (wersja koncertowa)

35 **B IX** **Rondo C-dur** na dwa fortepiany; **Wariacje D-dur** na 4 ręce; *dodatek* – wersja robocza Ronda C-dur (na jeden fortepian)

36 **B X** **Pieśni i piosnki**

37 **Suplement** Utwory częściowego autorstwa Chopina: Hexameron, Mazurki Fis, D, D, C, Wariacje na flet i fortepian; harmonizacje pieśni i tańców: „Mazurek Dąbrowskiego", „Boże, coś Polskę" (Largo), Bourrées G, A, Allegretto A-dur/a-moll

NATIONAL EDITION OF THE WORKS OF FRYDERYK CHOPIN

Plan of the edition

Series A. WORKS PUBLISHED DURING CHOPIN'S LIFETIME

1 **A I** **Ballades** Opp. 23, 38, 47, 52

2 **A II** **Etudes** Opp. 10, 25, Three Etudes (Méthode des Méthodes)

3 **A III** **Impromptus** Opp. 29, 36, 51

4 **A IV** **Mazurkas (A)** Opp. 6, 7, 17, 24, 30, 33, 41, Mazurka in a (Gaillard), Mazurka in a (from the album La France Musicale /Notre Temps/), Opp. 50, 56, 59, 63

5 **A V** **Nocturnes** Opp. 9, 15, 27, 32, 37, 48, 55, 62

6 **A VI** **Polonaises (A)** Opp. 26, 40, 44, 53, 61

7 **A VII** **Preludes** Opp. 28, 45

8 **A VIII** **Rondos** Opp. 1, 5, 16

9 **A IX** **Scherzos** Opp. 20, 31, 39, 54

10 **A X** **Sonatas** Opp. 35, 58

11 **A XI** **Waltzes (A)** Opp. 18, 34, 42, 64

12 **A XII** **Various Works (A)** Variations brillantes Op. 12, Bolero, Tarantella, Allegro de concert, Fantaisie Op. 49, Berceuse, Barcarolle; *supplement* – Variation VI from "Hexameron"

13 **A XIIIa** **Concerto in E minor** Op. 11 for piano and orchestra (version for one piano)

14 **A XIIIb** **Concerto in F minor** Op. 21 for piano and orchestra (version for one piano)

15 **A XIVa** **Concert Works** for piano and orchestra Opp. 2, 13, 14 (version for one piano)

16 **A XIVb** **Grande Polonaise in E♭ major** Op. 22 for piano and orchestra (version for one piano)

17 **A XVa** **Variations on "Là ci darem" from "Don Giovanni"** Op. 2. Score

18 **A XVb** **Concerto in E minor** Op. 11. Score (historical version)

19 **A XVc** **Fantasia on Polish Airs** Op. 13. Score

20 **A XVd** **Krakowiak** Op. 14. Score

21 **A XVe** **Concerto in F minor** Op. 21. Score (historical version)

22 **A XVf** **Grande Polonaise in E♭ major** Op. 22. Score

23 **A XVI** **Works for Piano and Cello** Polonaise Op. 3, Grand Duo Concertant, Sonata Op. 65

24 **A XVII** **Piano Trio** Op. 8

Series B. WORKS PUBLISHED POSTHUMOUSLY

(The titles in square brackets [] have been reconstructed by the National Edition; the titles in slant marks // are still in use today but are definitely, or very probably, not authentic)

25 **B I** **Mazurkas (B)** in B♭, G, a, C, F, G, B♭, A♭, C, a, g, f

26 **B II** **Polonaises (B)** in B♭, g, A♭, g♯, d, f, b♭, B♭, G♭

27 **B III** **Waltzes (B)** in E, b, D♭, A♭, e, G♭, A♭, f, a

28 **B IV** **Various Works (B)** Variations in E, Sonata in c (Op. 4)

29 **B V** **Various Compositions** Funeral March in c, [Variants] /Souvenir de Paganini/, Nocturne in e, Ecossaises in D, G, D♭, Contredanse, [Allegretto], Lento con gran espressione /Nocturne in c♯/, Cantabile in B♭, Presto con leggierezza /Prelude in A♭/, Impromptu in c♯ /Fantaisie-Impromptu/, "Spring" (version for piano), Sostenuto /Waltz in E♭/, Moderato /Feuille d'Album/, Galop Marquis, Nocturne in c

30 **B VIa** **Concerto in E minor** Op. 11 for piano and orchestra (version with second piano)

31 **B VIb** **Concerto in F minor** Op. 21 for piano and orchestra (version with second piano)

32 **B VII** **Concert Works** for piano and orchestra Opp. 2, 13, 14, 22 (version with second piano)

33 **B VIIIa** **Concerto in E minor** Op. 11. Score (concert version)

34 **B VIIIb** **Concerto in F minor** Op. 21. Score (concert version)

35 **B IX** **Rondo in C** for two pianos; **Variations in D** for four hands; *addendum* – working version of Rondo in C (for one piano)

36 **B X** **Songs**

37 **Supplement** Compositions partly by Chopin: Hexameron, Mazurkas in F♯, D, D, C, Variations for Flute and Piano; harmonizations of songs and dances: "The Dąbrowski Mazurka", "God who hast embraced Poland" (Largo) Bourrées in G, A, Allegretto in A-major/minor

Okładka i opracowanie graficzne · Cover design and graphics: MARIA EKIER
Tłumaczenie angielskie · English translation: JOHN COMBER

Fundacja Wydania Narodowego Dzieł Fryderyka Chopina
ul. Okólnik 2, pok. 405, 00-368 Warszawa
www.chopin-nationaledition.com

Polskie Wydawnictwo Muzyczne SA
al. Krasińskiego 11a, Kraków
www.pwm.com.pl

Wyd. I. Printed in Poland 2019. Drukarnia REGIS Sp. z o.o.
05-230 Kobyłka, ul. Napoleona 4

ISBN 83-920365-6-5

FRYDERYK CHOPIN
POLONAISES
published posthumously

Performance Commentary
Source Commentary (abridged)

PERFORMANCE COMMENTARY

Remarks concerning the musical text

Variants furnished with the term *ossia* were marked thus by Chopin himself; variants without this term result from discrepancies in the text between sources or from the impossibility of an unequivocal reading of the text.
Minor authentic differences (single notes, ornaments, slurs and ties, accents, pedal signs, etc.) which may be regarded as variants are given in round brackets ( ), editorial additions in square brackets [ ].
Performers with no interest in source-related problems and wishing to rely on a single text without variants are advised to follow the text given on the main staffs, whilst taking account of all markings in brackets.
Chopin's original fingering is marked with slightly larger digits in Roman type, **1 2 3 4 5**, distinct from editorial fingering, which is written in smaller italics, *1 2 3 4 5*. Where Chopin's fingering is given in brackets, the sources in which it appears provide no guarantee of its authenticity.
Indications of the division between the right and left hands, marked with a broken line, are given by the editors.
General problems regarding the interpretation of Chopin's works will be discussed in a separate volume entitled *Introduction to the National Edition*, in the section 'Problems of Performance'.

Abbreviations: R.H. – right hand; L.H. – left hand.

The tempos of the polonaises

The *Polonaises* contained in the present volume carry no authentic tempo indications or metronome markings. Of some help in finding appropriate tempos may be the following observations concerning markings that appear in *Polonaises* prepared by Chopin for print:
— verbal expressions range from **Maestoso** and **Allegro maestoso**, through **Allegro**, to **Allegro molto** or **Allegro con brio**. Characteristically, Chopin restricted himself on several occasions to indicating the type of dance (**alla Polacca** or **tempo di Polacca**), probably regarding the tempo of polonaises as well established and generally familiar;
— Chopin gave authentic metronome markings in three polonaises of a virtuosic character: *Alla polacca* from the *Variations in B♭*, Op. 2 and the *Polonaise in C*, Op. 3, and the *Polonaise in E♭*, Op. 22 (from bar 17). All three have the tempo ♩ = 96, which is the natural tempo for a danced polonaise;
— in two cases (*Polonaises in C# minor* and *E♭ minor*, Op. 26) the *Trio* has the expression **meno mosso**.
To sum up, the tempos of Polonaises should not range too far from the tempo of the dance (♩ = 96). This applies in particular to the first three, childhood, polonaises, as well as to works and sections of a virtuosic character. Lyrical works and sections may be taken more slowly. Cf. notes on the tempos of polonaises in the commentary to the volume of *Polonaises* in series A (6 **A VI**).

Pedalling

Pedal markings in Chopin's youthful works, including the majority of the *Polonaises* in the present volume, are generally given at the beginning of sections with a similar texture. In such cases they should be treated as exemplary, and an analogous pedalling should be applied to the further course of the work. In sections without any pedal signs, a harmonic pedal may be applied, its density matched to the texture and character of the music.

1. Polonaise in B flat major, WN 1

A *legato* articulation is recommended for the whole work, with the following exceptions:
— R.H. part in the introduction (bars 1-4),
— L.H. part in bars 33-36,
— notes marked with *staccato* dots.

Short grace notes (written as small semiquavers), the execution of which is not given, are best performed in an anticipated manner, that is, prior to the striking of the L.H.

2. Polonaise in G minor, WN 2

The chords in bars 1-2 & 13-14 should be performed, as far as possible, *legato*. Other passages using chordal technique, as well as all places with repetitions, sound more natural played *staccato* or *portato*. Besides this, a *legato* articulation is advised for the whole work.

p. 14 *Bars 8 & 17* R.H. The grace note f^2 at the beginning of bar 17 should be executed simultaneously to the L.H. The other two grace notes in these bars are best executed in an anticipated manner, that is, prior to the corresponding third in the L.H.

3. Polonaise in A flat major, WN 3

p. 18 *Bars 40, 45 & analog.* R.H. The turn in bars 45 & 58 should be executed analogously to the figure on the 3rd beat of bar 40. In both places the following procedure may be employed to facilitate performance (bar 45 an octave higher):

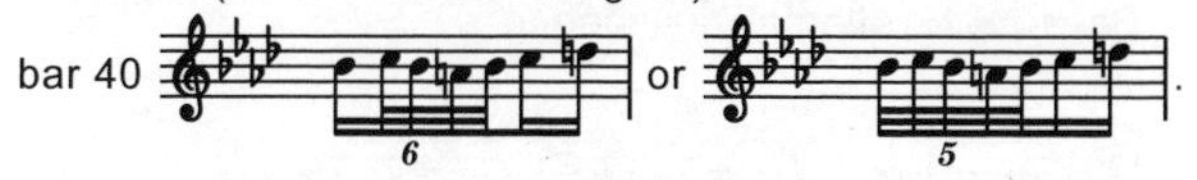

Bar 42 & analog. R.H. A more stylish execution is to strike the first of the grace notes together with the third in the L.H.

4. Polonaise in G sharp minor, WN 4

In the sources from which this Polonaise is familiar, additions, and possibly also changes, were undoubtedly made to the performance markings. The markings chosen by us create a picture of the composition that is relatively coherent, musically convincing and not contrary to the way in which Chopin usually marked his works. In other words, Chopin could have specified such an execution of this Polonaise, but there is no certainty that he did. Therefore, a greater flexibility is admissible in the interpretation of markings; where it is justified, they may be supplemented, and even modified.

p. 20 *Bar 14* R.H. Execution of the figure with the turn:

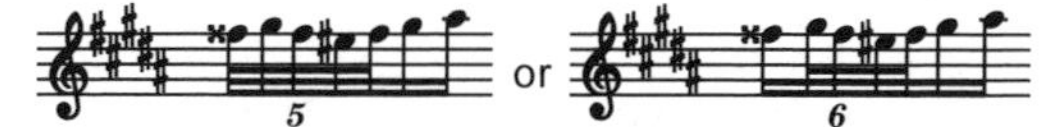

Bar 15 R.H. Two ways of executing the turn:

In the editors' opinion, the former gives a more natural phrasing.

p. 21 *Bar 34* R.H. The execution of the passage on the 2nd quaver may be facilitated as follows:

p. 22 *Bar 40* R.H. The grace note e^2 should be performed simultaneously with *F#* in the L.H.

Bar 49 L.H. In the event of difficulty with spanning the seventh at the beginning of the bar, the following fingering may be used:

5. Polonaise in B flat minor, WN 10

p. 24 *Bar 1 & analog.* R.H. The grace note should be played together with the L.H. octave.
R.H. In the last triplet the lower note of the 1st sixth is easier to execute with the L.H., striking on the 6th quaver the octave f-f^1.

Bar 8 & analog. R.H. Execution of the figure at the beginning of the bar:

e^1 together with the L.H. octave.

Bar 9 R.H. The grace note at the beginning of the bar should be played simultaneously with the 1st quaver of the L.H.

Bar 13 R.H. Alternative fingering:

etc.

p. 25 *Bar 15* R.H. The first of the grace notes $g\flat^1$ should be struck simultaneously with the L.H. *A♭*.

p. 26 *Bar 44* R.H. Execution of the turn:

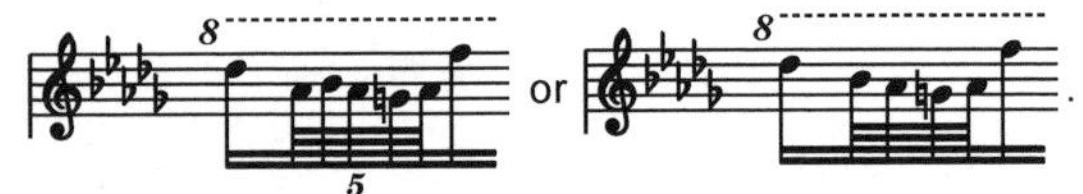

6. Polonaise in D minor, WN 11

Performance markings – see note at the beginning of the commentary to the *Polonaise in G# minor*, WN 4.

p. 28 *Bars 5, 7 & analog.* R.H. The grace note at the beginning of the bar should be struck simultaneously with the L.H. octave.
R.H. Execution of the trills:

(at the end of the bar a group of four or six notes may be played).

Bar 9 R.H. The grace notes may be executed either in such a way that the first in each pair is struck together with the L.H.,

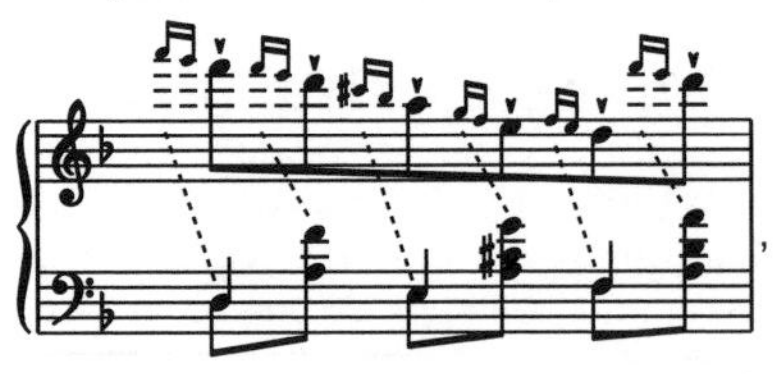

or else in an anticipated manner, prior to the simultaneous quavers in the two hands:

p. 30 *Bars 26-27* R.H. The term *legatissimo* certainly signifies here 'harmonic legato' (sustaining the chord members with the fingers):

etc.

p. 31 *Bars 48, 50 & 52* L.H. 'Harmonic legato' may be used here (see previous comment):

Analogously in the other 2 bars.

p. 33 *Bar 68* R.H. The grace notes should be played more quickly than the semiquaver triplets in the bars before and after (e.g. as demisemiquavers). A more stylish execution is to begin them simultaneously with the corresponding note in the L.H. (this applies to the 1st and 3rd figures), as long as this does not blur the difference in the execution that results from the notation of the figures in this bar and the next.

7. Polonaise in F minor, WN 12

The double grace notes in bars 8, 38, 54, 75 & 93 should be executed in such a way that the first is struck simultaneously with the corresponding note or dyad in the L.H. Such an execution is also advisable in bar 77, although in order to avoid a rhythmic deformation of the semiquavers of the lower voice, an anticipated execution is also admissible in this case.

p. 34 *Bar 13 & analog.* R.H. The start of the trill with grace notes:

f simultaneously with the *B♭* in the L.H.

p. 38 *Bar 78* R.H. Chopin's fingering does not signify here simply sliding the finger off the key, but is an 'expressive fingering', suggesting a *portato* articulation and a slight deceleration in order to emphasise the accented note $c\flat^2$. Chopin used this type of fingering more than once, e.g. in the *Nocturne in G minor*, Op. 37 No. 1, bar 6.

Bars 85, 86 & 88 R.H. The grace notes are best struck simultaneously with the corresponding quaver in the L.H.

8. Polonaise in B flat major, WN 17

The double grace notes in bar 9 & analog. and bar 16 should be executed as the ending of the previous melodic note, that is, in an anticipated manner.

p. 40 *Bar 17 & analog.* R.H. The first note of the arpeggio, d^1, should be struck simultaneously with the L.H. octave.

p. 41 *Bar 23 & analog.* R.H. Execution of the ornaments:

Bar 24 & analog. R.H. The grace note $e\flat^2$ at the beginning of the bar is best struck simultaneously with the L.H. chord.

Bar 24 R.H. The repeat of bars 1-24 may be treated *ad libitum*.

Bars 24-31 R.H. The trills are best executed as groups of five notes (without terminations –). The trills above the upper notes of the thirds in bars 25, 27, 29 & 31 may also be executed as mordents.

Bars 26, 28 & 30 R.H. Possible fingerings of the trill terminations:

bars 26, 28 

bar 30 or .

p. 43 *Bars 56-57 & analog.* R.H. All the grace notes in these bars are best executed in an anticipated manner, so as not to blur the distinctiveness of the leaps in the melodic line.

9. Polonaise in G flat major, WN 35

Performance markings – see note at the beginning of the commentary to the *Polonaise in G♯minor*, WN 4.

p. 46 *Bars 9, 11 & analog.* R.H. The trill may be executed without a termination – , or as a turn – .

Bar 11 & analog. R.H. The grace note $b\flat^2$ at the beginning of the bar should be struck simultaneously with the L.H. octave.

p. 49 *Bar 66* The editors are of the opinion that the ***f*** should not be overexposed in this place. It is not certain that the sign should not occur until this bar – cf. analogous bars 116-117.

Bar 67 & analog. R.H. The grace note $b\flat^2$ at the beginning of the bar may be either anticipated or executed simultaneously with the bass note.

p. 51 *Bar 102 & analog.* R.H. The grace notes at the beginning of the bar should be struck simultaneously with the bass notes.

Jan Ekier
Paweł Kamiński

SOURCE COMMENTARY /ABRIDGED/

Initial remarks

The present commentary in abridged form presents an assessment of the extent of the authenticity of sources for particular works, sets out the principles behind the editing of the musical text and discusses all the places where the reading or choice of the text causes difficulty. Posthumous editions are taken into account and discussed only where they may have been based on lost autographs or copies thereof. A precise characterisation of the sources, their relations to one another, the justification of the choice of basic sources, a detailed presentation of the differences appearing between them, and also reproductions of characteristic fragments of the different sources are all contained in a separately published *Source Commentary*.

Abbreviations: R.H. – right hand; L.H. – left hand. The sign → indicates a relationship between sources, and should be read as 'and the source(s) based thereon'.

The editing of the works in series B

Compared with the works intended and prepared for print by Chopin (National Edition series A), the works contained in the volumes of series B present a range of specific editorial problems. Their common underlying cause is the fact that the composer did not seek to publish these works, and so was not faced with that final moment of reflection regarding their exact notation.
As a result we encounter, on the one hand, works barely sketched or still being elaborated, for example without performance markings. Today these autographs are often inaccessible, and the only extant sources are either copies or editions prepared from such copies; these usually contain additions and amendments, the extent of which it is difficult to establish. In this situation the NE editorial team aim to reconstruct authentic sources. Depending on the state of sources, reconstruction may involve all elements of a work, including, in extreme cases, form, or else only some elements, such as all or a particular group of performance markings.
On the other hand, there also occur compositions for which we have several autographs, meticulously prepared but differing in many crucial details, written at different times, with a distinct lack of care taken over the final selection among many different ideas. In such cases it becomes necessary to give more than one of the variant versions of a work.
The variety of the sets of sources for particular works and the complex and uncertain relations among them oblige the editors to treat each work individually and to apply the editorial methods adopted with greater flexibility.
The notation of repeats. In both working autographs and those presented as gifts or mementos, Chopin sought the utmost economy in notating sections occurring several times, marking reiterations by means of repeat signs and markings such as *da capo* (*dal segno*) *al fine*. In works intended by Chopin for print, meanwhile, this type of short notation is applied solely to the main parts of a work, and a similar principle is therefore adopted in the works of series B, with the remaining repeats written out in full.
The resolving of editorial problems in series B by reference to analogous situations in chronologically and stylistically related works from series A is a general principle.
Authentic pedal markings occur only rarely, generally together with wider-ranging virtuoso or accompaniment figurations requiring the use of pedal to supplement the harmony. Where this type of texture encompasses a passage of several bars or more, the pedalling is quite often notated only at the beginning of the passage. Following similar principles, we supplement the markings wherever the sources are lacking in reliable pedalling and reduce their number in relation to sources where such markings are too numerous, that is, where those that could have been written by Chopin were certainly supplemented.
The execution of ornaments. In works belonging, by dint of their simplicity and brevity, to repertory of a primarily pedagogic character, we give the execution of ornaments directly by the musical text, and not in the *Performance Commentary*.

The chronology of the *Polonaises* of series B

All the *Polonaises* contained in the present volume date from Chopin's childhood and youth, preceding the earliest of the *Polonaises* prepared for print by the composer personally (Opp. 22 & 26). This clear division into two groups is without analogy in other Chopin genres: mazurkas and waltzes not published by Chopin were written over the whole period of his creative activity, parallel to those which he intended for publication. The two groups of *Polonaises* therefore complement one another in a particular way, together representing a clear cross-section of Chopin's entire output from the *Polonaise in B♭*, WN 1, his first extant essay in the genre, to the *Polonaise-Fantaisie*, Op. 61, one of the masterpieces crowning the last period of his work.
Previous collective editions present the *Polonaises* in the order in which they were found and published, which gives a completely chaotic picture in this respect.
The matter is complicated by the fact that the chronology of the *Polonaises* contained in the present volume is not precisely defined in the subject literature, and in several cases there occur discrepancies and errors. Hence the need for a brief discussion of this problem.
The *Polonaises in B♭*, WN 1, and *in G minor*, WN 2. The common opinion that the young Chopin's first work was the *Polonaise in G minor* is contradicted by a comparison of the pianistic means employed in the two compositions:
— the *Polonaise in B♭* contains no simultaneously struck octaves, which might have caused difficulties for a child's hands (in the *Polonaise in G minor* they appear several times);
— the bolder use of chordal technique in the *Polonaise in G minor*;
— the *Polonaise in B♭* lacks a virtuosic element, such as the impressive G minor arpeggio repeated several times in the *Polonaise in G minor*.
The *Polonaises in D minor*, WN 11, and *in F minor*, WN 12. The dating of these *Polonaises* raises crucial difficulties, as Chopin probably resumed work on them several times.
In the case of the *Polonaise in D minor*, this is indicated by the clash between the relatively modest range of textural means, not yet venturing far beyond those employed in the *Polonaise in G# minor*, and the considerably more mature harmony, particularly in the second part of the *Trio*. It is significant that in the notation of the earliest redaction of the *Polonaise*, this section of the *Trio* – if not entirely absent – was not notated directly after the section before it.
The earlier date of the start of Chopin's work on the *Polonaise in F minor* (*c.* 1826) results from certain graphical features of the script in the working autograph of the first redaction. Meanwhile, a reference in a letter written by Chopin in Nov. 1829 (see quotations *about the Polonaises...* before the musical text) speaks of the preparation of the autograph on the basis of another autograph (fair copy?) already in existence.
To summarise, we give below the chronology of the composing of the *Polonaises* that we regard as the most probable:

Polonaise in B♭	WN 1	1817
Polonaise in G minor	WN 2	2nd half of 1817
Polonaise in A♭	WN 3	Apr. 1821
Polonaise in G# minor	WN 4	1824
Polonaise in B♭ minor	WN 10	July 1826
Polonaise in D minor	WN 11	1825-1827
Polonaise in F minor	WN 12	1826-1828 (-1829?)
Polonaise in B♭	WN 17	1829
Polonaise in G♭	WN 35	Oct./Nov. 1830

The order of the *Polonaises* in the present volume corresponds to the chronology given above.

1. Polonaise in B flat major, WN 1

Sources
[A] An autograph was most probably never produced.
EM Józef Elsner's manuscript written probably in the first half of 1817 to the dictation of the little Chopin playing the *Polonaise* (original

lost, photocopy in the Fryderyk Chopin Institute Library, Warsaw). It was hitherto believed to be the manuscript of Chopin's first teacher, Wojciech Żywny, or the composer's father, Mikołaj Chopin*. This manuscript was the base text – directly or indirectly – for all previous editions of the *Polonaise* (the earliest edition hitherto uncovered is Leon Chojecki's teaching arrangement published in *Nowości Muzyczne*, 3, L 664 Ch, Warsaw 1910).

Editorial principles
We give the text of **EM**. For teaching purposes we give the execution of ornaments directly by the text.

p. 12 *Bar 10* R.H. In **EM** the grace note g^3 erroneously has the form of a small quaver. Cf. bar 6, and also 8 & 25.

p. 13 *Bar 23* R.H. In **EM** the *staccato* dot is missing above the 1st quaver. Cf. bars 24, 29 & 30.

Bars 37-42 In **EM** these bars are marked as a repeat of bars 27-32.

Bar 42 In **EM** the return of the main part of the *Polonaise* following the *Trio* is not marked. At the time, this repetition was considered obvious, and so the lack of the relevant indication in the manuscripts of Chopin's *Polonaises* is the rule rather than the exception.

2. Polonaise in G minor, WN 2

Sources
[M] No manuscript (autograph?) has been preserved.
PE Polish edition prepared from **[M]** by the firm of Rev. J. J. Cybulski, Warsaw, Nov. 1817 (see quotations *about the Polonaises...* before the musical text). The NE editorial team has tracked down three copies of this print, two of which show traces of handwritten annotation.
PEB Copy of **PE** with Chopin's own note on the last page: 'Ofiaruję ten Polonoise J. Białobłockiemu. Autor.' [I offer this Polonoise to J. Białobłocki. The composer] (Main Library, Academy of Music, Katowice). Also visible are hand-written corrections made on the cover (presumably also by Chopin), incl. the deletion of the words 'faite' and 'Musicien'. There are no changes to the musical text.
PEX Copy of **PE** with numerous handwritten** corrections to the musical text, comprising a quite thorough proofreading of this print (Österreichische Nationalbibliothek, Vienna). It is difficult today to state who made these corrections, although it cannot be excluded that Chopin himself corrected the first edition of his work for his own use or with the intention of offering it to someone.

This *Polonaise* is included by the NE among the group of posthumous works, since, given the composer's young age, it is impossible to speak of his intention to publish the piece or – taking into account the number of errors – of any control over the preparation of its publication.

Editorial principles
We adopt as the base text **PE**, correcting probable errors (most in accordance with corrections in **PEX**). The change written into **PEX** in bar 22 is included as a variant. For teaching purposes we give the execution of ornaments directly by the text.

p. 14 *Bars 1-2 & 13-14* R.H. The function of the curved lines between the chords is not entirely certain: whilst in bars 1-2 they are almost certain to apply to the common note d^1, in bars 13-14 they may apply either to the common inner note (f^1) or else to the lower notes of the chords, in which case they would be motivic slurs for the pairs of chords. However, in the whole of the *Polonaise* there appear only ties, and slurs which are part of the markings of irregular groupings (the situation is similar in the autograph of the *Polonaise in A♭*, WN3, and the probable autograph of the *Polonaise in D minor*, WN11). Therefore, it seems much more likely that these lines should be read as ties.

Bar 2 R.H. **PE** erroneously has *b♭* as the lower note of the 1st chord. The error was corrected in **PEX**.

Bars 5 & 9 R.H. In **PE** the lines linking the notes d^3 are placed over the stems. However, their function as ties is beyond doubt.

Bar 8 R.H. As the grace note, **PE** erroneously has $e\#^3$. Most editions have left the height of the note and changed the chromatic sign to ♭ or ♮. However, it seems much more likely that the error was in the placement of the note head (as many as seven such errors were made in the *Polonaise*) rather than the use of the chromatic sign; $c\#^3$ is also supported by the more natural hand position, especially for a small (child's) hand.

Bar 11 L.H. As the last quaver **PE** erroneously has f^1-a^1, which we alter to the harmonically smoothest $e\flat^1$-a^1. An identical correction is written into **PEX**.

Bar 12 L.H. In **PE** the lowest note of the chord on the 2nd quaver is erroneously f^1, which in **PEX** is altered to d^1. Cf. bars 22 & 30.

Bar 19 R.H. Comparison with the analogous bar 21 suggests the unwitting omission here of a tie sustaining *F*. A tie was written into **PEX**.
R.H. On the last semiquaver of the 2nd beat **PE** erroneously has *F* (cf. analogous motif in bar 21). The error was corrected in **PEX**.

Bar 22 R.H. The main text is the printed version of **PE**, the variant in the footnote is the handwritten amendment to **PEX**. This alteration cannot be seen as the correction of an error, as the printed text is entirely correct. Characteristic of the motivic pattern of the typical polonaise ending occurring here are both the repetition of the melodic note (a^1 in the main text) and the halting of the motion on the upper leading note (c^2 in the variant).

p. 15 *Bar 25* R.H. In **PE** the pitch of the 7th and 8th semiquavers is not entirely certain, as these notes are placed a little too high and at first glance can be read as f^2 and g^2. In **PEX** the placement of the two notes was corrected.

Bar 35 L.H. Missing on the 2nd quaver in **PE** is the lower note of the chord, *f*. The error was corrected in **PEX**.

Bar 38 L.H. **PE** erroneously has *b♭* as the middle note of the chord on the 2nd quaver (cf. analogous bar 30). In **PEX** the error was corrected.
In **PE** the return of the main part of the *Polonaise* following the *Trio* is not marked. Cf. note to *Polonaise in B♭*, WN 1, bar 42.

3. Polonaise in A flat major, WN 3

Sources
A Autograph with dedication for Wojciech (Adalbert) Żywny, dated 23 Apr. 1821 (Warsaw Music Society). This is the earliest extant Chopin autograph. The title page and the first page of the musical text are written out very carefully in ink, but the second page already contains several corrections made without due care over calligraphy. In addition, visible throughout the manuscript are the now faded traces of a detailed proofreading made in pencil. In spite of the serious difficulties encountered in identifying and interpreting some of the amendments, the style of notation and the character of those changes still legible allow one to see in them a later (by at least several months) redaction of the work by the composer. In this situation it may be doubted whether this autograph was ever actually presented to Żywny by his brilliant pupil. All previous editions of the *Polonaise* took account of the ink text of **A** alone (the earliest known edition was prepared by J. Michałowski for the firm of Gebethner & Wolff, G 2515 W, Warsaw 1901).

* For a lengthy justification of the identification of Elsner as the author of this manuscript, see J. Ekier, 'Four communiqués on the work on the National Edition', in *Chopin In Performance: History, Theory, Practice* (Warsaw, 2004).
** The editors of the National Edition are grateful to Dr Andrea Harrandt of the Österreichische Nationalbibliothek, Vienna, for confirming this fact.

Editorial principles

We give the text of **A**, taking account of the layer of the latest pencil corrections made by Chopin. The text of the original version, written in ink, is given in the appendix (pp. 55-57). This makes it easy to locate the final-phase changes when comparing the two versions. We alter enharmonic notes notated contrary to the orthography.

p. 16

Bar 1 R.H. The pitch of the last note raises doubts: beneath the note placed at the pitch of $a\flat^3$ (the highest note in bars 1-2) only three ledger lines are added, which gives f^3. It may be assumed that Chopin first wrote the notes (heads and stems), distributing them in accordance with the shape of the melodic line he heard in his head, and then added the ledger lines, generally 'by intuition', without counting them (this is supported by later autographs, in which errors in the number of ledger lines are by far the most common among mistakes over the pitch of notes). This clearly indicates that $a\flat^3$ was the pitch Chopin intended for this note.

Bar 3 L.H. The notes $a\flat^1$ in the chords were added to the thirds of the original version only in bars 1-2. In these bars Chopin also changed the 1st quaver, deleting the upper $a\flat$. Both these changes should doubtless be treated together, as part of a comprehensive modification of the accompaniment pattern. Since the $a\flat$ on the 1st quaver was also deleted in bar 3, it is most likely that the supplement to the following quavers should also apply to this bar.

Bar 6 R.H. Chopin wrote the penultimate semiquaver as $d\flat^2$.

Bars 9-10 L.H. The marks that appear in these bars on the 3rd beat are not entirely clear. We give the most likely reading of the clearer addition in bar 10 and adopt an analogous solution for bar 9.

Bars 13-38 The uncertainty regarding the repetition of these bars is caused by the placement in **A** of two repeat signs between bars 12-13. The first closes bar 12, the last in the system, whilst the second opens bar 13 at the beginning of the following line. Such an arrangement of signs at the transition between systems is generally used to indicate the repetition of both the preceding section and the section that follows. However, the second sign in **A** is not, as we would expect, turned towards bar 13 (‖:), but is an exact replica of the first (:‖). The doubts could be dispelled by the sign at the end of bar 38, but since bars 27-38, a repeat of bars 1-12, are not written out, an attempt to arrive at the end of the section encompassed by the possible repeat leads back to the same place (at the end of bar 12). In this situation it is difficult to determine whether the 11-year-old Chopin needlessly doubled the repeat sign for bars 1-12, or else unskillfully marked the repetition of bars 13-38. The inconsistent marking of the repetition of certain sections also occurs in a similar context in the autographs of both Op. 26 *Polonaises*.

Bar 15 L.H. A barely legible sign appears at the beginning of the bar. It may possibly relate to a change of the 1st quaver from $B\flat$ to f.

Bar 16 L.H. The signs on the 2nd beat are difficult to read. The solution presented combines the simplicity and logic of the accompaniment with a high degree of graphical convergence with the visible additions. Another, stylistically less likely, version is

p. 17

Bar 20 R.H. Written in ink on the 2nd quaver is $a\flat^1$, which, given the $a\flat^1$ struck simultaneously by the L.H. is an obvious mistake (cf. also analogous motif in bar 16). In this case, therefore, the pencil alteration is simply the correction of an error.
R.H. The unclear addition on the 5th quaver may denote an additional $d\flat$.

Bar 23 L.H. Instead of $f\flat^1$ Chopin continues to write e^1 in the chords.

Bars 27-38 These bars are marked in **A** as a repeat of bars 1-12.

p. 18

Bars 40 & 44 R.H. On the 6th semiquaver **A** has $g\flat^2$.

Bar 47 L.H. The main text and the variant of the 1st half of the bar are two ways of reading the barely visible pencil mark in **A**.

Bars 47-49 R.H. The notes $b\flat^1$ on the 4th and 5th quavers are only added in bar 47. However, taking into account the construction and character of the motifs in these bars, it seems highly unlikely that this addition was intended to apply to this bar alone.
L.H. The unclear annotation at the end of bar 47 may denote a change of the last quaver from f^1-a^1 to $g\flat^1$-a^1. If this were the case, then the alteration would most probably apply also in bars 48-49. This possibility is included here in the form of variants.

Bars 52-59 In **A** these bars are marked as a repeat of bars 39-46.

Bar 59 In **A** the return of the main part of the *Polonaise* following the *Trio* is not marked. Cf. note to *Polonaise in B♭*, WN 1, bar 42.

4. Polonaise in G sharp minor, WN 4

Sources

[A] Lost autograph, supposedly offered to Louise Du-Pont (Dupon).

[PC] Lost copy of **[A]**, produced as a base text for the first Polish edition. The preparation of a separate manuscript was necessary if only because recurring passages that in **[A]** were doubtless indicated in short were written out in the edition in full. In addition, the copy probably included revisions to the text, incl. the supplementing of performance markings.

PE First Polish edition, Josef Kaufmann (20), Warsaw 1864, probably based on **[PC]**. It is furnished with the following note: 'As far as one may deduce from the manuscript and its dedication, this composition was written by Fryderyk Chopin in his 14th year, and has not been previously printed anywhere'.

CX Copy of a fragment of the work (up to bar 39) made by a person unknown (Fryderyk Chopin Museum, Warsaw). The text of **CX** is essentially convergent with **PE**, such that, in spite of the different layout (bars 20-27 are marked as a repeat of bars 5-12) and a number of other minor discrepancies, **CX** appears to be a copy of this edition, prepared for practical purposes (the presence in **CX** of an almost identical informational note seems telling).

GC Copy produced by an unknown person as a base text for the first German edition (Schott co. archive, Mainz). Based on **[A]** or **[PC]**, it displays a considerable number of mechanical errors and inaccuracies. Numerous engraver's annotations are visible.

GE First German edition, les fils de B. Schott (17943.), Mainz 1864. **GE** transmits the corrected text of **GC**.

Editorial principles

We adopt as the base text **GC**, compared with **PE**, as the sources probably closest to the autograph. We reduce the number of pedal signs, bringing them in line with the density of markings found in authentic sources of other youthful Chopin works.

p. 19

Bar 1 The sources give **Moderato** as the tempo indication. We regard it as inauthentic, since part of the performance markings that appear in the sources was certainly added by a foreign hand, and the *Polonaises* from Chopin's childhood and youth that are contained in the present volume carry no tempo markings in any of the sources that were not subjected to editorial alteration.
f appears only in **GC** (→**GE**).

Bars 5-10 & analog. L.H. In **GC** the slurring is imprecisely marked (bars 7, 10, 20-25 have no slurs at all). We give the slurring of **PE**.

Bar 9 ***p*** appears only in **GC** (→**GE**).

Bar 12 & analog. The performance markings in this bar raise a number of doubts:

— on the 2nd quaver instead of ***fz*** **GC** has *Sec* (**PE**: *sec.*) – a term which Chopin never used. The unjustified use of a capital letter allows one to infer a misinterpretation of the sign ***fz***, readily used by Chopin and often misread by copyists and engravers.
— on the 2nd beat the sources have the term *rubato*, incomprehensible in this context (the rhythmic formula at the end of a period that was characteristic of the polonaise was not marked in this way by Chopin in any of the other 20 or so works or fragments of a polonaise character).
— ***p*** appears only in **PE**.

p. 20 *Bar 13* We omit *a tempo*, meaningless without the *rubato* in bar 12.

Bars 13-15 The sources give *grazioso* in bar 13 and *espressivo* in bar 15. The use of both these terms within such a short section of uniform melody seems unlikely to have come from the composer. The greater doubts are raised by *grazioso*, used on two further occasions in the *Polonaise* in different grammatical forms (*con grazia* in bar 5, *graziosamente* in bar 40).

Bar 15 R.H. The main text comes from **GC** (→**GE**), the variant from **PE**. Most probably one of the versions is wrong, but available sources do not allow us to state which one.

Bars 18-19 R.H. The slur is split in the sources into two (**PE**) or three (**GC**) parts. In uniform progressions of this sort consecutive slurs denoted simply a *legato* articulation. As they have no bearing on the construction of motifs or phrases, we replace them with a single slur, in line with the modern-day understanding of these signs.

p. 21 *Bar 28* Instead of ***f*** and *energico* **PE** has here ***p***. This marking most probably comes from the editor's revision (by analogy with bar 50). Although the authenticity of the markings in **GC** (→**GE**) is uncertain, they are well suited to the virtuoso panache of this section of the *Trio*, confirmed by the signs ***f*** in bars 32 & 36 (***p*** in bar 50, as a dynamic variant appearing after a three-bar diminuendo that adds variety to the flow of the *Trio*, raises no reservations).

Bar 36 Instead of the ***f*** in **PE**, **GC** (→**GE**) has *energico*. In the analogous bar 58 all the sources have ***f***. Since in **[A]** bars 51-61 were presumably marked as a repeat of bars 29-39, we unify the marking, giving that which appears most often.

Bar 38 R.H. On the 1st beat **PE** erroneously has the rhythm ♪.♬.

Bars 38 & 60 R.H. The main text comes from **GC** (→**GE**), the variant from **PE**.

p. 22 *Bar 43* L.H. At the beginning of the bar **GC** erroneously has *d#*.

Bar 45 We alter the ***sfz*** not used by Chopin to ***fz***.

p. 23 *Bar 52* L.H. As the 1st quaver **GC** (→**GE**) erroneously has *d#*.

Bar 61 In **PE** the return of the main part of the *Polonaise* following the *Trio* is not marked. Cf. note to *Polonaise in Bb*, WN 1, bar 42.

5. Polonaise in B flat minor, WN 10

Sources

[A] Autograph, presented to Wilhelm Kolberg, already lost by 1877, when, following Wilhelm's death, his brother Oskar unsuccessfully tried to find it (see quotations *about the Polonaises...* before the musical text). Information contained in one of the letters cited indicates that the preparation of **[A]** was probably preceded by the sketching of the *Polonaise* just before Chopin left for Duszniki in July 1826, when this work was composed. A copy produced from **[A]** (**KC1**, see below) suggests that this autograph, though legible, was notated in haste and in short.

KC1 Copy of **[A]** produced by Oskar Kolberg at the beginning of the 1860s ('about 18 years ago', as Kolberg wrote in December 1878), now lost, familiar from a photocopy (Österreichische Nationalbibliothek, Vienna). Visible on the musical text are numerous deletions, corrections and additions, resulting from Kolberg's editing of the *Polonaise*, doubtless while preparing it for print in 1878. These adjustments primarily involved varying the texture, harmony, rhythm and ornamentation, as well as diversifying sets of similar passages appearing next to one another. Their aim was to lend the *Polonaise* a more polished form, more attractive for the publisher. The reiterations of lengthier sections are not written out, which undoubtedly accords with the notation of **[A]**. One is struck by the quite numerous rhythmic errors, involving the writing out of overlarge values for notes and rests.

[KC2] Lost fair manuscript, prepared by Oskar Kolberg from **KC1** as the base text for the first Breitkopf & Härtel edition. The existence of this manuscript is testified in Kolberg's correspondence (see quotations *about the Polonaises...* before the musical text). In **[KC2]** Kolberg made further adjustments to the *Polonaise*: most of the changes introduced in **KC1** are reproduced, others are omitted, and some are taken further, e.g. in bars 8, 45-49 (especially 48) and 53-57.

GE First German edition, Breitkopf & Härtel (C. XIII. 16.), Leipzig Jan. 1880, based on **[KC2]**. The *Polonaise* was included in volume 13 (Posthumous Works) of a collected edition prepared by Bargel, Brahms, Franchomme, Liszt, Reinecke and Rudorff ('Erste kritisch durchgesehene Gesammtausgabe').

PE First Polish edition, *Echo Muzyczne*, 12 (June 1881), ed. Jan Kleczyński. The text is based on **GE**, with fingering added.

Editorial principles

The known circumstances surrounding the composing of the *Polonaise*, the preparing of a copy of the autograph and its later disappearance, and also the preparing of the first, posthumous edition, lead to the conclusion that **[A]** was the only authentic source of the text of the work. The deciphering of the deletions and additions made by Kolberg in **KC1** allow us to reconstruct, with a large degree of probability, the text of **[A]**. This version, simpler in its sound and technical demands, appears to be more in keeping with the occasional character of the work. Therefore we adopt as the base text **KC1**, according to its state prior to the introduction of changes.

p. 24 *Anacrusis–bar 1* R.H. After Kolberg's alterations **KC1** (→**[KC2]** →**GE**) has the following version of the beginning: . It is significant that the original version of this place was not altered in its repetition written out as the start of the repeat of the 1st eight-bar period.

Anacrusis–bar 8 We mark the repetition of these bars by means of a repeat sign, in line with Chopin's practice (cf. all other *Polonaises* in this volume). They were similarly marked in **GE**. In **KC1** the repetition is written out (in a simplified form): bars 1 & 8 in full, bars 2-7 marked with bar lines (empty).

Bar 1 & analog. R.H. The version we give of the 6th quaver of bar 1 was changed by Kolberg in **KC1** (→**[KC2]**→**GE**) to the following:

. In **KC1** this version also appears – uncorrected – in the written-out repeat of bar 1 (cf. previous comment). The full notation of the repeat of this bar is presumably the work of Kolberg (cf. last paragraph of comment to bars 53-57), who in the place in question immediately notated the arbitrary version he had introduced himself. It is significant that in bar 25, the last bar written out in this section of the *Polonaise* (as a signal for the repeat of bars 1-8), the original version is preserved unchanged.

Bars 1-2 & analog. R.H. In **KC1** (→**[KC2]**→**GE**) the notes *bb*¹ at the transition between the bars are tied. The authenticity of this tie is highly dubious: the repeated notes play a crucial role in the melody of this section of the *Polonaise* in general, and in the preceding triplet motifs in particular.

Bar 2 & analog. R.H. In the last chord **KC1** has a deleted note $b\flat^1$ tied to the $b\flat^1$ in the previous chord. As a musically unjustified complication of the notation, these elements were presumably added, and subsequently removed (they do not appear in **GE**), by Kolberg.

Bars 2 & 4 and analog. R.H. **KC1** has the grace note $g\flat^2$ before the last quaver of bar 2 and $d\flat^2$ before the 1st quaver of bar 4. Both appear to have been added by Kolberg, who later relinquished them in [**KC2**] (→**GE**).

Bars 2-3 & analog. R.H. The tie sustaining f^1 appears only in **KC1**. It gives a smoother transition from the octave doublings of the melody (bar 2) to the third doublings (bar 3).

Bar 4 & analog. R.H. Kolberg gave the second half of the bar the following forms: **KC1**  **GE** .

Bar 6 & analog. R.H. Due to deletions, **KC1** has only $a\flat^1$ as the demisemiquaver. A similar version appears in **GE**.
R.H. Deleted on the 5th quaver in **KC1** is $d\flat^1$. This version also appears in **GE**.

Bar 8 & analog. On the 2nd quaver **KC1** erroneously has rhythmic values twice as great in the parts of both hands.
L.H. Instead of the rests closing the bar **GE** has the opening motif of the *Polonaise* shifted down an octave.

Bar 9 R.H. On the 5th quaver **KC1** has a dotted rhythm. Certain graphical features of the notation seem to testify that the dot extending the 1st note and the beam reducing the 2nd were added by Kolberg. The even semiquavers of **GE** can therefore be seen as a return to the authentic version.

Bars 9-12 L.H. As the 4th quaver **KC1** erroneously has $e\flat$ (4 times).

Bars 11-12 R.H. In **KC1** all the rests erroneously have the value of semiquavers.

Bar 14 R.H. On the 2nd quaver **KC1** erroneously has the rhythm 𝅘𝅥𝅮. 𝅘𝅥𝅯.

p. 25

Bar 15 R.H. Missing in **GE** is the 1st grace note $g\flat^1$.
R.H. It is difficult to state whether the sign *tr* deleted in **KC1** appeared in [**A**] or was added by Kolberg. In **GE** it is absent.

Bars 15-16 L.H. The version of the accompaniment given by us was altered by Kolberg in **KC1** (→[**KC2**]→**GE**) to the following (the notes in parentheses appear only in **GE**):

Bar 17 L.H. On the 2nd quaver **GE** has even semiquavers.
R.H. Visible above the note a^2 in **KC1** (→[**KC2**]→**GE**) is a turn sign. We omit it, as it seems much more likely to have been added by Kolberg.

Bars 18-20 L.H. Due to changes made by Kolberg, **KC1** (→[**KC2**]→**GE**) has the following version:

(The notes in parentheses appear only in **KC1**. On the last quaver of bar 20 **GE** has the octave $B\flat$-$b\flat$ instead of the chord.)

Bar 21 Visible above the part of the R.H. in **KC1** are some deleted additions by Kolberg, who seems to have attempted to supplement Chopin's copied out text. Ultimately, this bar had the following form in **GE**: 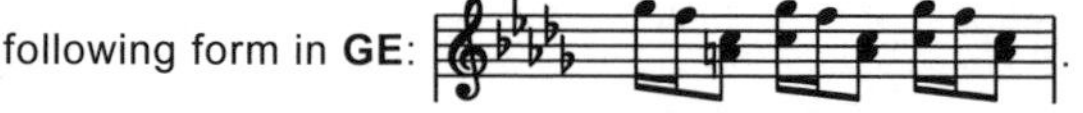.

Bar 22 In this bar Kolberg made increasingly far-reaching alterations:

Bar 23 L.H. In **KC1** (→[**KC2**]→**GE**) the highest note in the last chord was changed to c^1.

Bar 24 R.H. The second half of the bar after Kolberg's alterations in **KC1** (→[**KC2**]→**GE**):  (the note in parenthesis appears only in **KC1**).

p. 26

Bars 35-42 & 51-57 R.H. Giannetto's Cavatina from Act I of Rossini's *La gazza ladra* (the original is in D major), the theme of which Chopin used in the *Trio**:

Bars 35-44 In **KC1** this passage is framed by repeat signs. We omit them, as most probably later additions by Kolberg.

Bar 35 L.H. In **KC1** (→[**KC2**]→**GE**) the 1st quaver was shifted down an octave ($D\flat_1$-$D\flat$). The compass of the pianos that Chopin had at his disposal when writing the *Polonaise* reached only to F_1.

Bar 37 L.H. In **KC1** (→[**KC2**]→**GE**) the quavers filling the 2nd beat were replaced by a crotchet.

Bar 38 L.H. In **KC1** (→[**KC2**]→**GE**) the last chord was replaced by a rest.

Bars 41 & 57 L.H. After the changes made by Kolberg in **KC1** (→[**KC2**]→**GE**) the accompaniment gained the following form:

(The tie in parenthesis appears only in **GE**.)

Bar 42 R.H. In **GE** the bottom three notes of the chord on the 2nd quaver have the value of a quaver, such that this edition has only f^2 as a demisemiquaver.

* We give the text of the aria after *F. F. Chopin, Opere*, in: *Polacche*, ed. Franco Luigi Viero (Milan: Edizioni del Cygno, Corsico 2002).

Bars 43-44 & 59-60 L.H. On the 1st quaver of bar 44 **KC1** has an additional note *a♭*, tied to the *a♭* in the last chord of bar 43. A tie sustaining *a♭* also appears between the 4th and 5th quavers of bar 43 (bars 59-60 are not written out). We regard them as probably later additions by Kolberg. In **GE** the accompaniment took on the following form: .

Bars 45-49 In these bars Kolberg made increasingly far-reaching alterations:

We give the text of **KC1** according to its pre-revision state.

p. 27

Bars 51-54 L.H. Visible in this passage are a number of changes made in **KC1** (→[**KC2**]→**GE**):

— on the 5th quaver of bar 51 and the 1st quaver of bars 52-54 the octave $B\flat_1$-$B\flat$ was replaced by the single note $B\flat$;

— on the 4th quaver of bars 52 & 54 the chord f-$b\flat$-$d\flat^1$ was replaced by the chord $d\flat$-f-$b\flat$;

— in bar 52 the last chord f-$b\flat$-$d\flat^1$ was transferred to the 5th quaver (instead of the octave $B\flat_1$-$B\flat$), and a rest was placed on the 6th quaver;

— in bar 53 the last chord was changed to $g\flat$-a-c^1-$e\flat^1$.

Bar 52 R.H. In **KC1** the first 2 notes were changed by Kolberg from crotchets to quavers.

R.H. In **KC1** (→[**KC2**]→**GE**) the last quaver was replaced by the following figure: .

Bars 53-57 R.H. In **KC1** & **GE** Kolberg gradually added notes filling in the harmony:

Some explanation is required of the notation of bar 56 (up to the 1st quaver of bar 57) in **KC1**. Certain graphical features of the notation suggest that [**A**] ended on the first strike of bar 56, which was followed by an understood repetition of bars 40-44. In **KC1** Kolberg, probably in order to notate the lower voice he had added, wrote one more bar, merely sketching the upper voice (there are no dotted rhythms on the 3rd beat of bar 56).

Bar 55 L.H. In **KC1** the 3rd quaver was shifted down an octave.

Bar 60 R.H. Added to the last 2 sixths in **GE** are the tied notes $a\flat^2$.

6. Polonaise in D minor, WN 11

Sources

AI Manuscript – probably an autograph – comprising bars 1-47 with no performance markings (lost, repr. in supplement to *Ilustrowany Kurier Codzienny* of 24 Sept. 1934). Today it is difficult to state whether the single page that is visible on the extant photograph constitutes the whole of the manuscript, or whether the 2nd part of the *Trio* was written on a lost 2nd page. **AI** displays certain original features, in both appearance (more frequent use of quaver flags than beams, one-voice notation of bars 18 & 20) and substance (above all a simplified version of bars 1-4 & 5-8).

[**A**] Lost, presumably working, autograph, containing a later version of the work than **AI**. It served as the basis for the copy of Mikołaj Chopin and perhaps, after possible corrections and additions made by the composer, for the lost copy of Fontana, as well.

CMC Copy attributed to the composer's father, Mikołaj Chopin, doubtless based on [**A**] (Fryderyk Chopin Museum, Warsaw). **CMC** contains quite numerous errors, most often due to the confusion of graphically similar sections appearing next to one another.

[**CF**] Lost copy produced by Julian Fontana as the base text for the edition of Chopin's posthumous works that he was preparing. It is difficult to state which source Fontana had at his disposal in writing out [**CF**]. It may have been [**A**], especially if Chopin made certain alterations to it after **CMC** had been produced; the existence of another autograph is also a possibility. It is almost certain that Fontana made some changes to the work he was copying, primarily supplementing performance markings and writing out all the repeats in full, but also not refraining from interference in the areas of pitch and rhythm. An assessment of the scope of these changes and their possible authenticity is a complex and delicate matter; among other things, account must be taken of a declaration made by Fontana in his afterword to the posthumous edition of Chopin's works: 'not only did I hear the composer play almost all the works in this collection many times, but [...] I also performed them for him, preserving them in my memory ever since just as he created them [...]'.

FEF Fontana's French edition, J. Meissonnier Fils (J. M. 3528), Paris July 1855, most probably based on [**CF**]. Fontana made final editorial adjustments when proofreading **FEF**.

GEF Fontana's German edition, A. M. Schlesinger (S. 4397), Berlin July 1855, doubtless based on **FEF** or a proof thereof. In **GEF** the *Polonaise* was given an inauthentic opus number: Op. 71 No 1.

EF = **FEF** & **GEF**. Minor discrepancies exist between the two versions of Fontana's edition, raising doubts over their mutual relations; however, given the lack of essential differences, this has no great bearing on establishing the text.

Editorial principles

We adopt as the base text **EF**, compared with **CMC** to eliminate probable errors and those of Fontana's alterations which are of questionable authenticity. Where more crucial differences occur, we refer to the version of **AI**. We sift through performance markings with particular rigour, leaving only those which are musically essential and convergent in type and number with markings in other Chopin works of this period.

p. 28

Bar 1 **EF** has the certainly inauthentic metronome marking ♩ = 84 (in **GEF** erroneously ♪). Also, the tempo indication *Allegro maestoso* in the same source was probably added by Fontana (cf. comment to *Polonaise in G# minor*, WN 4, bar 1).

Bars 1-2 R.H. In **CMC** the notes e^1 on the 5th quaver are extended by extra stems to the value of a crotchet.

Bars 1-4 Introduction in the version of **AI**:

Bars 3 and 9 & 34 R.H. *Staccato* markings appear only in **C**MC.

Bar 4 R.H. In **C**MC the notes a^1 in the first two chords are tied.

Bars 5-6 & analog. R.H. In **C**MC the last $g\#^2$ in bar 5 is tied to the $g\#^2$ at the beginning of bar 6.

Bars 5-8 & analog. R.H. In **AI** bars 5-6 have the following form:

Bars 7-8 are marked only as a repeat, an octave higher, of bars 5-6.

Bar 8 & analog. L.H. The crotchet stem on the first *c#* appears only in **C**MC. We also add it to the *c#* on the 5th quaver, where **C**MC erroneously has the sign ***tr***.

Bar 10 & analog. R.H. The slur over the thirds appears only in **GE**F.

Bar 11 & analog. L.H. The octave on the 4th quaver is notated in **C**MC as a semiquaver, which is followed by a rest.

Bars 13-26 Doubts are raised by the dynamic markings in **E**F in these bars:
— ***sf*** (on the 3rd quavers in bars 13-16 and on the 2nd quavers in bars 22-23) was used by Chopin only exceptionally;
— the combination of ***f*** at the beginning of bar 17 and *sempre* ***f*** in bar 18 seems superfluous;
— the contrasts produced by ***pp*** in bars 20 & 26 seem excessive (the manipulation to which the dynamic markings were being subjected even during the proofreading of **FE**F is confirmed, for example, by the visible trace of a change in this edition of ***ff*** to ***f*** in bar 26).
We introduce changes aimed at notating those elements of the dynamic conception of **E**F which may be authentic in a manner in keeping with Chopin's usage as documented in other works.

Bars 14-16 & 19 The fingering in parentheses may be authentic; it comes from **E**F.

p. 29

Bar 16 L.H. On the 4th quaver **AI** has a semiquaver triplet as in the preceding bars.

Bar 17 R.H. In **C**MC the note b^3 on the 3rd quaver is notated as a semiquaver, which is followed by a rest.

Bars 18 & 20 L.H. **C**MC erroneously has *a#* as the lower note of the chords on the 2nd, 4th and 6th quavers.
L.H. The main text comes from **E**F, the variant from **AI** & **C**MC. Although the contour of the bass line in bars 18-21 is not as regular in the main version as in the variant, it is more closely correlated to the figures of the R.H. – more static in bars 18 & 20, more mobile in bars 19 & 21. This version is technically somewhat easier.

Bar 24 L.H. At the beginning of the bar **AI** has an additional note *c#* in the chord (analogously to the beginning of bar 23), whilst **C**MC – perhaps by mistake – has the octave A_1-A.

Bars 24 & 25 R.H. The main text comes from **E**F, the variant from **AI**. We give both versions, as the similarity of the neighbouring figures may possibly have led to mistakes in the sources. One version that is certainly wrong is that of **C**MC, which has g^1 in bar 24 and a^2 in bar 25.

Bars 25-26 L.H. Beginning with the 2nd quaver of bar 25, **AI** has 6 times the octave *A-a*, which is doubtless the original version of this place. Meanwhile, the version of **C**MC – 5 octaves A_1-A (as in the preceding bar) and the seventh a-g^1 at the beginning of bar 26 – is probably wrong.

p. 30

Bar 29 L.H. At the beginning of the bar **AI** has the octave A_1-A.

Bars 30-37 In **AI** & **C**MC these bars are marked as a repeat of bars 5-12.

p. 31

Bar 38 The term *Trio* appears only in **AI**.

Bars 42-43 & 78-79 In **E**F accents also appear on the 2nd and 3rd beats of bar 42. This seems to be an inauthentic addition:
— the melodious section of the theme beginning with the syncopation in bar 41 would return too soon to the clearly marked crotchet pulse that dominated before it (from the beginning of the *Trio*);
— the motif of three accentuated crotchets appears several times over the course of the *Trio*, in bars 46, 49, 51, 56 & 68;
— the accents in bar 43 are confirmed, as it were, by the figures of the L.H., resembling the motifs of the introduction.

Bars 43 & 79 R.H. The note g^1 on the 3rd beat appears only in **AI** & **C**MC.

Bars 47 & 83 R.H. In **C**MC the second *g-a* in the first two chords is tied.

Bar 48 We replace the marking ***mf***, only occasionally used by Chopin, with the term *espressivo*.

Bar 50 R.H. **C**MC has the following rhythm: .

Bar 53 R.H. In **E**F the crossing of voices on the 2nd beat was not marked: the g^2 in the upper voice is a crotchet, while both the $a\#^1$ and the g^1 are quavers and belong to the lower voice.

Bar 55 R.H. In **E**F the octave $c\#^1$-$c\#^2$ is detached from the chord and has the value of a dotted minim. As this alteration was only made during the printing of **FE**F, it cannot be Chopin's.

Bar 61 We give the version of **C**MC, correcting the $c\#^2$ erroneously notated in the 2nd figure to $b\#^1$ (in **[A]** it was most likely c^2). The version of **E**F contains questionable elements in the parts of both the L.H. (*F#* at the beginning of the bar) and the R.H. ($b\#^2$ and $b\#^1$ in the dyads opening the 1st and 3rd figures). The harmonic progression used in bars 60-62 appears many times in Chopin's works (e.g. *Rondo in C minor*, Op. 1, bars 59-61, and *Lento con gran espressione*, WN 37, bars 1-2; cf. also *Polonaises in G# minor*, WN 4, bars 14-16, and *in B♭ minor*, WN 10, bars 30-32), always with the characteristic semitone step of the bass in the last two chords. This reduces to a minimum the possibility that the quaver *F#* in the bar in question may be authentic. As regards the R.H. figures, it seems inconceivable that Chopin would drop here the appoggiaturas with which, from the preceding bar, he melodically and harmonically embellished the main figurate motif of the *Trio*. Situations in which the suspension of one of the members of a chord is notated as an altered form of another (here b^2 & b^1 to the $b\#^1$ & *b#* of the chord) often induced the editors of Chopin's works to revise, cf. e.g. note to *Ballade in G minor*, Op. 23, bars 45 & 47, or *Ballade in F minor*, Op. 52, bars 164-165.

Bar 62 R.H. As the 1st semiquaver **C**MC has only $e\#^1$. The incomprehensible two-voice notation of this single note points to the possibility of an error in this source. Some later collected editions arbitrarily give the fourth $e\#^1$-a^1 as the 1st semiquaver.

Bars 62 & 66 The notes f## are notated in the sources as g.

Bar 64 R.H. The main text comes from **E**F, the variant from **C**MC. Both versions seem possible:
— the harmonic progression in the variant version develops in a most natural way (used as a transitional note in the cadence leading to C# minor in bar 65 is e^2); cf. analogous bars 66-67;
— the $e\#^2$ in the main text suggests a return to the C# major chord which (bar 62) was the point of departure for this whole modulatory section; the unexpected resolution to C# minor in bar 65 acts as an impulse to further modulation.

Bar 67 The main text of the 2nd beat comes from **E**F, the variant from **C**MC.
R.H. The change of the highest note in the last figure proposed by the editors assumes an error in the notation or reading of [**A**].

p. 32 *Bar 69* R.H. We give the first figure after **C**MC. In **E**F it is written an octave lower, most probably due to a mistake in specifying the scope of the *all'ottava* sign.

Bar 72 L.H. At the beginning of the bar **C**MC has only the lower A_1.

7. Polonaise in F minor, WN 12

Sources

AI Working autograph of an earlier redaction (private collection, photocopy at the Fryderyk Chopin Institute Library, Warsaw). Judging from the style of notation, this may be the first version of the *Polonaise*. **A**I bears traces of corrections, some of which are believed to have been made later, e.g. when copying out the work to present someone with a commemorative autograph.

[**A**1] Lost autograph presented to Eliza Radziwiłłówna (see quotations *about the Polonaises...* before the musical text).

A2 Fair autograph, produced – according to a note in Chopin's hand – in Stuttgart, in 1836, and presented to a person unknown (Fryderyk Chopin Museum, Warsaw).

FEF Fontana's French edition, J. Meissonnier Fils (J. M. 3530), Paris July 1855, probably based – through a lost copy made by Fontana – on **A**I prior to certain corrections being made. In editing the *Polonaise*, Fontana also included a number of unquestionably authentic elements either drawn from other (lost) sources (e.g. [**A**1]) or simply remembered (cf. excerpt from the afterword to **FE**F quoted in the characterisation of the same edition of the *Polonaise in D minor*, WN 11). Other alterations, including the supplementation of performance markings and the writing-out of reprises, are most probably inauthentic. **FE**F also contains several clear errors.

GEF Fontana's German edition, A. M. Schlesinger (S. 4399), Berlin July 1855, doubtless based on **FE**F or a proof thereof. In **GE**F the *Polonaise* was given an inauthentic opus number: Op. 71 No 3.

EF = **FE**F & **GE**F. Minor discrepancies exist between the two versions of Fontana's edition, raising doubts over their mutual relations; however, given the lack of essential differences this has no great bearing on establishing the text.

Editorial principles

We reproduce the text of **A**2, correcting a small number of minor inaccuracies. The earlier redaction of the work, reproduced on the basis of **A**I & **E**F, is given in an appendix (pp. 58-63).

p. 35 *Bars 25 & 71* L.H. Missing in **A**2 is the dot extending the minim *d♭*. As this was most probably due to oversight, we give the dot, after **A**I.
R.H. In **A**2 the division between the hands was marked as follows:

Bars 26 & 72 R.H. In **A**2 the quaver g^1 on the 2nd beat erroneously has two extending dots.

Bars 29-34 L.H. It is not entirely certain what *staccato* marks Chopin intended for the bass notes at the beginning of these bars. Most (bars 30-32 & 34), however, clearly resemble wedges, and it is this option that we adopt for all six bars.

p. 36 *Bars 37-39* L.H. Missing in **A**2 are the naturals raising *d♭* to *d* in bar 37 and $d\flat^1$ to d^1 in bars 38-39, and also the ♭ lowering *g* to *g♭* on the 6th quaver of bar 37. The corresponding signs in the R.H. part and the harmonic sense leave no doubt that the lack of these signs results from an oversight on Chopin's part.

Bars 46-50 R.H. In **A**2 the function of the curved lines linking the minims *c* with the following quavers of the same pitch is not entirely clear: their shape and placement suggest ties, whilst the *staccato* dots clearly indicate the need to strike these quavers.

p. 37 *Bars 51-72* In **A**2 these bars are marked as a repeat (*dal Segno*) of bars 5-26.

p. 38 *Bar 73* L.H. In **A**2 the scope of the slur is not clear: it might also end on the 3rd or 4th quaver.

p. 39 *Bar 88* R.H. **A**2 has only one ♮ before the last third on the 2nd beat. The sign is of such dimensions that it could apply to both the upper and the lower note. Yet there is no doubt as to the need here for naturals before both notes.

Bar 90 R.H. Missing in **A**2 before the 2nd beat is the ♭ restoring $e\flat^1$.

Bars 91-98 In **A**2 these bars are marked as a repeat (*Trio da Capo*) of bars 73-80.

8. Polonaise in B flat major, WN 17

Sources

[**A**I] Lost working autograph of an earlier redaction, from which copies were made by both Ludwika Jędrzejewiczowa and Julian Fontana (lost). A considerable number of errors common to the two copies indicates the difficulty in reading [**A**I], doubtless caused by deletions and corrections.

[**A**] Lost fair autograph from which the first Polish edition of the *Polonaise* was prepared. [**A**] was doubtless offered to someone as a keepsake, as is indicated by the abundance of precise performance markings, characteristic of many Chopin autographs of this type (cf. e.g. *Polonaise in F minor*, WN 12). In relation to the version of [**A**I] it contains a number of clear improvements (the most important in bars 3, 57-58, 74, 82-84), including a correction of chromatic orthography (6th quaver of bar 58).

JC Copy of Ludwika Jędrzejewiczowa (Fr. Chopin Museum, Warsaw), made from [**A**I]. It contains a large number of errors and inaccuracies. Several minor revisions may have been made by Chopin.

PE First Polish edition, J. Chrząszcz (no plate number), Żytomierz, c. 1853, based on [**A**]. **PE**, lithographed by the Warsaw firm of M. Fajans, contains a large number of mechanical errors, yet at the same time it does faithfully reproduce the graphical appearance of the manuscript. This is testified by a number of characteristically Chopinian graphical devices, such as the notation of low positions in the R.H. on the lower staff, accents of various length and the terms *cresc.* (*dim.*) placed within the signs $<$ ($>$). The short notation used in this edition – *Dal Segno* – of recurring sections of the main part of the work (bars 38-51) and of the *Trio* (bars 88-103) is also concurrent with Chopin's script.

FEF Fontana's French edition, J. Meissonnier Fils (J. M. 3530), Paris July 1855, based – most probably via Fontana's (lost) copy – on [**A**I]. As it is very unlikely that Fontana could have had some other manuscript of the *Polonaise* at his disposal when preparing the base text, the only additional source of authentic elements in **FE**F were Fontana's personal contacts with Chopin (see Fontana's statement on this matter quoted in the characterisation of **FE**F of the *Polonaise in D minor*, WN 11). The discrepancies between **FE**F and **JC** can be ascribed to errors on the part of the copyists as well as additions and changes made by Fontana.

GEF Fontana's German edition, A. M. Schlesinger (S. 4399), Berlin July 1855, doubtless based on **FE**F or a proof thereof. In **GE**F the *Polonaise* was given an inauthentic opus number: Op. 71 No 2.

EF = **FE**F & **GE**F. Minor discrepancies exist between the two versions of Fontana's edition, raising doubts over their mutual relations; however, given the lack of essential differences, this has no great bearing on establishing the text.

Editorial principles

As the base text we adopt **PE**, compared with **JC** & **E**F to eliminate errors. In several cases this text is supplemented (in round brackets) by elements of **E**F whose possible authenticity raises no reservations.

The dedication comes from **PE**. The NE editors failed to uncover any information regarding its addressee. Moreover, it may possibly have been added by the publisher (dedications added arbitrarily by publishers were not uncommon at that time; we find them even in works published during Chopin's lifetime by Wessel of London).

p. 40 *Anacrusis* R.H. In **JC** the first *f* is written as a struck-through grace note tied to the *f* in the subsequent chord. The quaver rest written beneath this note indicates a probable error in the notation of the note.

Bar 1 In **PE** the dynamic sign looks like ***p***. However, it seems very likely that [**A**] could have had ***f*** here, as the following suggests:
— the placement of the sign on the stem of the 1st chord in the R.H., which may have made it difficult to read correctly;
— the shape of the sign, divergent from other ***p*** appearing in **PE**; the shape of its lower part resembles the sign ***f***;
— other performance markings in the introduction, especially the accents in bars 1-3 and the *marcato* in bar 4;
— the character, texture, register and key of the introduction.
EF also has here ***f***.

Bars 1-8 There is no doubt that the introduction was shaped over several stages, as is testified by the discrepancies among extant sources and analysis of the revisions visible in **JC**. Although the lack of an autograph precludes the exact recreation of all the changes, some of their key elements can be reconstructed:
— in the earlier sources (**JC** & **E**F), based on [**A**I], not all the bass notes are doubled in the lower octave; what is more, these sources differ in this respect:

In **JC** asterisks mark traces of effaced dotted minims *B♭*, *B♭* & *G*. This means that only in the stage of revision was the rhythm ♩ 𝅗𝅥 in bars 1-3 introduced and the bass note at the transition between bars 3 & 4 changed from *G* to *B*. This notation, and possibly also other changes in [**A**I], doubtless simplified and imprecise, proved not entirely comprehensible to copyists. The discrepancies referred to here resulted from corrections made on top of a short notation – as in **JC** – of the octaves. Throughout this passage we give in the L.H. the octaves consistently written in **PE** and raising no doubts with regard to either sources or style.
— at a later stage of revision – in [**A**] (→**PE**) – Chopin made further improvements in bars 3 & 8 (see below, comment to these bars).

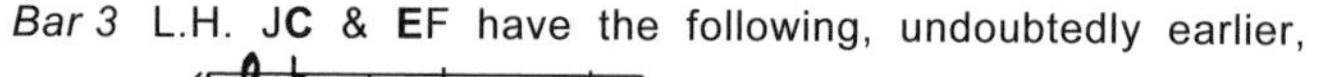

Bar 3 L.H. **JC** & **E**F have the following, undoubtedly earlier, version:

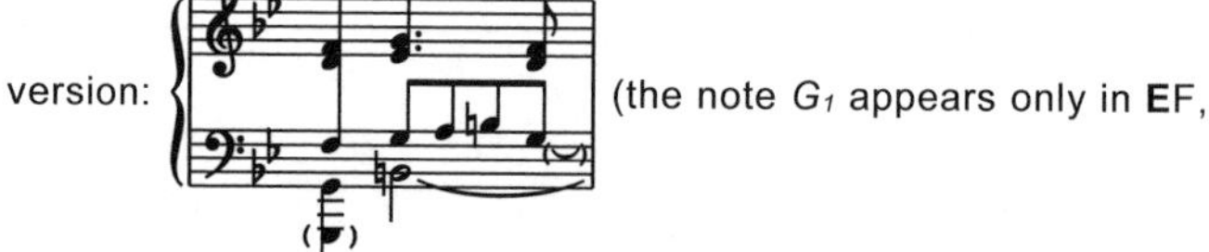

(the note G_1 appears only in **E**F, and the tie sustaining *g* only in **JC**). Incongruous in this version is the combination of the first two chords and the doubling of the leading note *b-B* on the 5th quaver of the bar.
R.H. **PE** erroneously has c^1 as the lower note of the semiquaver at the end of the bar.

Bar 6 R.H. On the 3rd beat **JC** & **E**F have even quavers.

Bar 8 L.H. At the beginning of the bar **JC** & **E**F have an extra *f*. In combination with the preceding bar this gives a parallel shifting of the chord, *B♭-b♭-*d^1*-*f^1 to *F-f-a-*c^1 (these sources are lacking the note $B\flat_1$ on the 3rd beat of bar 7, cf. comment to bars 1-7).

Bar 9 The marking ***p*** comes from **E**F. We give it here, as the lack of a new dynamic marking could be confusing after the ***f*** in bar 1. Moreover, the relevant sign may possibly have been overlooked by the engraver of **PE** (in this edition, bar 9 begins a new page; such a situation makes omissions more likely).

Bars 9, 17 & analog. R.H. On the 3rd beat **JC** & **E**F have even quavers.

Bars 10 & 37 L.H. On the 5th quaver **JC** & **E**F have *f* tied and *a-*$e\flat^1$ struck.

Bars 11 & 38 L.H. **JC** & **E**F have the following version:

Bars 12 & 39 L.H. On the 2nd quaver **JC** has the triad *b♭-*$e\flat^1$*-*g^1 in bar 12 and the sixth *b♭-*g^1 in bar 39. **E**F has the sixth in both bars. **PE** has here the chord *e♭-g-*$e\flat^1$, containing the note *e♭*, unquestionably wrong in this context. Taking into account the possibility in this situation of a mistake by the lithographer and also the harmonic content and voice-leading of the accompaniment, we regard the chord *g-b♭-*$e\flat^1$ as the most probable reconstruction of the version of [**A**]. Due to the conjectural character of this chord we give the version of **E**F in the variant.
R.H. In **JC** & **E**F the beginning of the bar has the following form:

Bars 12-13 & 39-40 R.H. Missing in **E**F are the ties sustaining d^2-f^2.

Bars 13 & 40 L.H. As the 2nd and 3rd strikes in the bar **JC** has the seventh *f-*$e\flat^1$, **E**F the chord *f-*c^1*-*$e\flat^1$.

Bars 14-15 & 41-42 R.H. The tie sustaining g^1 appears in **JC** & **E**F. Its absence in **PE** may be due to oversight on the part of the lithographer – very likely given the transition to a new line that occurs in this edition.

Bars 15 & 42 L.H. As the lower note of the 1st chord we give the *f* appearing in **PE**, which raises no doubts with regard to sources or style. **JC** & **E**F have here *e♭*, in **E**F tied to the *e♭* in the next chord. This note may result from a misreading of [**A**I] by the copyists, confused by Chopin's manner of writing vertically the notes forming a second, and presumably also its imprecise notation in [**A**I]. The tie of **E**F, not entirely understandable given the arpeggio sign embracing the entire 2nd chord, was probably not added until the printing stage.

L.H. In the 2nd chord **PE** has an additional c^1, which is doubtless a misreading of [**A**] (establishing the presence or absence of an inner note of a chord lying on a ledger line can be very problematic in Chopin's manuscripts; cf. e.g. comment to *Waltz in C# minor*, Op. 64 No. 2, bars 34, 42 & analog.).

Bars 16 & 43 L.H. In **PE** the grace note *e* is erroneously notated as *e#*. In **EF** it is entirely absent.
R.H. At the beginning of the bar **PE** erroneously has the octave d^1-d^2.

p. 41

Bars 19 & 46 R.H. The ***tr*** sign appears in **JC** & **EF**. We cannot exclude an oversight on the part of the lithographer of **PE**.

Bars 20 & 47 R.H. After the trill, **JC** & **EF** have only the crotchet g^1. We give the enhanced version of **PE**. A similar supplementing of the melody can be found, e.g., in the *Waltz in A♭*, WN 48, bar 14.

Bars 21-22 & 48-49 R.H. The sources have the following versions:

In the version of **PE** the rest at the beginning of bar 22 is doubtless an error, which we correct on the basis of the remaining sources.

Bars 23 & 50 R.H. At the beginning of the bar both **JC** and **EF** have erroneous versions:

This is probably due to the notation of [**AI**] being imprecise or difficult to read. In the version of **EF** we may also suspect a revision by Fontana. We give the version of **PE**, which raises no doubts.
L.H. In the 2nd chord **EF** has an additional f^2. The authenticity of this pianistically somewhat trickier version cannot be entirely ruled out, but the two other doubts regarding this bar incline one to consider this version, too, as not deriving from Chopin.
L.H. In **EF** the last *F* has the value of a crotchet. This may be due to a misreading of the unclear notation of [**AI**], as is indicated by the rhythmic error of **JC** in this place:

Bar 24 The repetition of bars 1-24 is marked clearly only in **EF**. The form of other Chopin *Polonaises* indicates that the notation of the remaining sources is probably inaccurate in this respect.

Bars 24, 26, 28 & 30 The trills on the 6th quavers are notated differently in each of the sources. **EF** has ***tr*** four times above the R.H., whilst in **JC** & **PE** the ornaments appear only in bar 24: ***tr*** for both hands in **JC** and ~~ above the R.H. in **PE**. Taking into account the quite frequent misunderstandings in interpreting Chopin's signs ***tr*** and ~~, we give in bar 24 ***tr***. In the subsequent bars we leave the repetition of the ornaments to the discretion of the performer.

Bars 25 & 27 R.H. On the 2nd quaver of bar 25 **PE** has ~~, and in bar 27 there is no ornament at all. These are certainly notational inaccuracies, and so we give in both bars ***tr*** , as in bars 29 & 31 and in line with **JC** & **EF**.

Bars 25, 27, 29 & 31 R.H. In **JC** & **EF** the rhythm of the motifs in thirds is differentiated and internally inconsistent:

This may be due to the imprecise notation of [**AI**], probably altered by Chopin.

Bars 26, 28 & 30 R.H. Missing in **JC** are the terminations of the trills in these bars, whilst **EF** has them in all three. It is difficult to state whether the lack of a termination in **PE** in bar 30 was an oversight or intended by Chopin.

Bars 31-32 R.H. In **EF** the notes c^2 & $e\flat^2$ are tied over.

Bars 33 & 34 R.H. Missing in the 1st chords in **JC** & **EF** are the notes c^1 and the ties binding them to the c^1 in the previous bars.

p. 42

Bars 36-37 L.H. The main text comes from **PE**, the variant is a version analogous to that of bars 9-10 & 17-18, and in these bars appears in **JC** & **EF**.

Bars 38-51 In **PE** – certainly after [**A**] – these bars are marked as a repeat (*D.S.*) of bars 11-24. In **JC** the repeat of bars 13-24 was notated in a similar way. In **EF** all such passages marked in abridged form were written out in full.

p. 43

Bars 52, 60 & analog. L.H. Before the chord on the 3rd beat, **EF** has an arpeggio sign. In **JC** such a sign appears only in bar 52.

Bars 52-53, 60-61 & analog. In some of these bars in **JC** & **EF** the notes *d* in the L.H. and d^1 in the R.H. that appear on the 2nd and 3rd beats are tied. **JC** has ties in the L.H. in bar 52 and in the R.H. in bar 60 (the same applies to bars 88 & 96, which are not written out in full), **EF** has them in both hands in bars 52, 53, 88, 89 & 96 and in the R.H. in bar 60. In [**AI**] ties most probably appeared in bars 52, 60 & analogous. However, judging from the version of **PE** adopted by us, it seems that in [**A**] Chopin decided to repeat these notes, marking with the term *tenuto* the need for them to be held precisely. Cf. bars 68-69.

Bars 53, 61 & analog. L.H. At the beginning of the bar **JC** & **EF** have additionally the grace note G_1 (as in the next bar).

Bar 56 & analog. L.H. On the 2nd quaver **JC** & **EF** have $b\flat^1$ as the highest note.

Bar 57 & analog. R.H. On the 2nd quaver **PE** has the third $e\flat^3$-g^3. This is doubtless a mistake.

Bars 57-58 & analog. **JC** has here the following, original version:

The version of **EF** differs from this only in the lack of the stem extending the *e♭* in bar 57, the presence of a tie sustaining the minim *d* in bar 58 and the sound of the 4th quaver of the L.H. in bar 58: $e\flat^1$ instead of c^1-d^1.

Bars 58, 70, 72 & 74-76 R.H. The fingering, possibly given by Chopin, appears in **EF**.

Bar 59 & analog. L.H. On the 5th quaver **JC** & **EF** have an additional semiquaver *d* tied over with the preceding minim.

Bar 63 & analog. L.H. As the 5th quaver **PE** erroneously has *e♭*.

Bar 64 & analog. L.H. On the 4th quaver **JC** has the chord a-c^1-a^1, **EF** the sixth a-$f\#^1$.

Bars 64-65 & analog. R.H. At the beginning of the 3rd beat **EF** is lacking the mordent above $b\flat^2$ ($b\flat^3$).

Bar 65 & analog. L.H. On the 6th quaver **PE** has $b\flat^1$ added in the chord. This is unquestionably an error, most probably left over from an inexact proofreading: in order to change $b\flat^1$ to d^2, the correct note has been added (d^2), but the wrong note has not been removed ($b\flat^1$). This type of 'half' correction occurs more than once in the first editions of Chopin works, cf. e.g. *Ballade in G minor*, Op. 23, bar 171 or *Scherzo in B minor*, Op. 20, bars 135 & 292.

Bar 67 & analog. L.H. Before the *D* at the beginning of the bar **JC** & **EF** have the grace note *C#*.
R.H. As the 5th semiquaver **EF** has *a*. The convergent version – with *f#* – of **JC** & **PE** points to an alteration by Fontana or simply an error. The authenticity of *f#* is confirmed by the precautionary ♮ that appears in **JC** & **EF** before a^1 on the 2nd beat.

p. 44

Bars 68 & 69 In **JC** & **EF** the octave *A-a* on the 2nd beat is tied over with the *A-a* on the 3rd beat.

Bar 70 R.H. In **PE** the tie sustaining $e\flat^4$ was omitted.

Bars 72-73 R.H. In **EF** the last quaver of bar 72 and the first of bar 73 are tied. **JC** has neither these ties nor that sustaining b^1.

Bar 74 L.H. As the bass foundation **JC** & **EF** have the octave *C-c*. We give the *D♭-d♭* of **PE**, certainly Chopin's. In this version, in respect to the whole-bar rhythm of bass changes, a stricter analogy is maintained with bars 70-71 & 74-75.
R.H. **PE** & **JC** do not have the tie sustaining $d\flat^4$. Also, in **PE** the *all'ottava* sign wrongly begins only with the demisemiquavers, and in **JC** it is entirely absent. **EF** has the correct version.

Bar 78 L.H. At the beginning of the bar **JC** & **EF** have only *E*.
R.H. At the end of the bar **EF** gives the trill termination $a\#^2$-b^2.

Bar 80 R.H. At the beginning of the bar **EF** has b^3. This may be a misreading of **[AI]** or a change made by Fontana, which, given the convergent version of **JC** & **PE**, may be considered arbitrary.

Bar 82 R.H. In the 1st quaver **JC** & **EF** have an extra *a*, as in the subsequent chords. The omission of this note in **PE** is undoubtedly an improvement characteristic of Chopin: it avoids doubling the third of the chord and makes it easier to expose the melodic note in the bass.

Bars 82 & 84 L.H. On the 4th quaver of bar 82 **JC** & **EF** have semiquavers (after a dotted crotchet at the beginning of the bar) instead of demisemiquavers. In bar 84 the semiquavers on the 4th quaver appear – after a quaver – only in **EF**.

p. 45

Bars 88-103 In **JC** & **PE** these bars are marked as a repeat (respectively *Dal Segno* & *TRIO dal Segno*) of bars 52-67.

Bar 103 In **EF** the repeat of the main part of the *Polonaise* after the *Trio* is entirely written out in notes. In the remaining sources this return – obvious in this form – was not marked in any way.

9. Polonaise in G flat major, WN 35

Sources

[A] Lost autograph, probably contained in the album of Tytus Woyciechowski (see quotations *about the Polonaises...* before the musical text). **[A]** was most probably the only authentic text of the work.

[KC] Lost copy of Oskar Kolberg, given to the editors of the periodical *Die Musik* (see quotations *about the Polonaises...* before the musical text). From Kolberg's correspondence we learn that this was copied not directly from **[A]**, but indirectly from some other copy. The arbitrary changes made by Kolberg in his copy of the *Polonaise in B♭ minor*, WN 10 (see commentary) allow us to suspect that he probably interfered in this *Polonaise*, as well (especially in the *Trio*) – an assumption which may be confirmed by the formulation used by Kolberg in his letter to Breitkopf & Härtel: 'It is my pleasure to enclose the *best* version [italics, NE] of the Chopin *Polonaise in G♭ major* circulating in various copies'.

[PE] First Polish edition, Josef Kaufmann, Warsaw, 1869-70, based on a lost copy. It remains an open question whether this copy was a direct transcription of **[A]**, although it is likely. There apparently existed two impressions of **[PE]**, which soon became very rare (see quotations *about the Polonaises...* before the musical text); today, not a single copy is known.

GC Copy prepared by an unknown copyist as the base text for the first German edition (Schott co. archive, Mainz). Presumably made from the base text of **[PE]**, it displays a considerable number of mechanical errors and inaccuracies. Numerous engraver's annotations are visible in **GC**.

GC' Fragment of **GC**, encompassing the main part of the *Polonaise* (bars 1-58), written out – due to some misunderstanding – a second time; this fragment was then deleted. Since this repetition could not have appeared in the authentic sources, the discrepancies between analogous fragments of **GC** & **GC'** arose solely due to inexact copying. As a result, an analysis of these differences allows us to eliminate some errors and omissions.

GE First German edition, les fils de B. Schott (20029.), Mainz 1870. **GE** transmits the revised text of **GC**.

Kle Second Polish edition, Gebethner & Wolff (G. W. 952), Warsaw 1882. The *Polonaise* was included in volume 3 of a collected edition of the works of Chopin prepared by Jan Kleczyński. Most probably based on **[PE]** or one of the lost copies, **Kle** was certainly revised by a foreign hand.

EDM Edition of the *Polonaise* in a sheet music supplement to an issue of the Berlin periodical *Die Musik* devoted to Chopin (Chopin-Heft), Oct. 1908. The text of this edition, based on [KC], differs in many details from the versions of the remaining sources (the most serious difference is the presence of bar 32). This testifies most probably the lack of a direct dependency of [KC] on copies used in the preparation of earlier editions.

Editorial principles

All the extant sources bear clear traces of inauthentic editorial alterations; outside interference is also almost certain to have occurred in the lost sources on which the extant texts were based. Therefore we encounter serious difficulties in reconstructing Chopin's text. As the basis of the text with regard to pitch and rhythm we adopt **GC** as probably the closest to an authentic source, compared with **EDM**, which probably transmits certain authentic details. As regards performance markings, we apply the following principles:
— we give markings that are convergent in both sources listed above; more specifically, we do not include the certainly inauthentic pedalling of **GC** (**EDM** gives no pedal markings);
— when various indications of a similar meaning appear in the same place, we adopt that which is closest to Chopin's practice in this respect; similarly, when the same markings appear in almost the same place, we place them where it is closest to the natural flow of the music;
— we give in brackets essential additions; round brackets signify that the addition appears in one of the sources, whilst square brackets are used for editorial additions (the exception here are pedal markings added without brackets).
Discussed below are only the most important issues relating to performance markings.

p. 46

Bar 12 R.H. On the 3rd beat **EDM** has the rhythm ♪𝄿𝅘𝅥𝅯, as in bar 10. In the analogous bar 42 all the sources have a dotted rhythm.

Bars 16 & 46 L.H. In the last chord, doubts concern the sound of the highest note: a^1 or $a\flat^1$. The notation of the sources provides no grounds for resolving this matter, as the authenticity of all the versions is open to question:
— a ♮ giving a^1 appears only in **EDM**, where it may have been added by the copyist or the publisher;
— in the remaining sources, given the ♮ raising $a\flat^2$ to a^2 in the R.H. the lack of a corresponding sign in the L.H. may be regarded as imprecise notation – so common in Chopin.

Neither do stylistic criteria allow us to make a clear choice between the versions. Both possibilities can be found in a similar harmonic context in Chopin, although in this place each version can be accused of a certain awkwardness:
— a^2 gives a parallel, octave progression with a doubling of the altered note; similar progressions appear, e.g., in the *Fantaisie in F minor*, Op. 49, bar 108 or the *Barcarolle*, Op. 60, bar 95. In the *Polonaise* one is disturbed by the delayed resolving of the note a^1 to $b\flat^1$, which does not appear until the 2nd beat of the next bar;
— $a\flat^2$ produces the simultaneous occurrence of the natural and altered fifth of the chord, such as we find, e.g., in the *Waltz in G♭*, WN 42, bar 56 or the *Fantaisie in F minor*, Op. 49, bars 104 & 273; in the *Polonaise* this juxtaposition sounds harsher due to the close position of the chord.
The version proposed by the NE editors, modelled on Chopin's idea applied in a similar context in the *Polonaise in C minor*, Op. 40 No. 2, allows all awkwardness in the voice-leading to be avoided in a tonally economical way.

Bars 19 & 49 R.H. As the 1st semiquaver of the 3rd beat **Kle** has in the lower voice the fourth $e\flat^2$-$a\flat^2$. Visible traces of the introduction of this version during proofreading show this to have been added by the editor, and its authenticity is highly unlikely.

Bars 21-22 The hairpins > in bar 21 appear only in **E**DM. The sign < in **GC** (→**GE**) & **Kle** appears – probably by error – in bar 23.

p. 47

Bars 22 & 52 L.H. On the 3rd beat in the lower voice we give the third *g♭-b♭* appearing in **E**DM. The remaining sources have here the third $b\flat$-$d\flat^1$, which, forming a pianistically awkward repetition with the following semiquaver $d\flat^1$, is probably wrong.

Bars 28 & 58 L.H. The first *d♭* has the value of a minim, given by us here, in **E**DM. In the remaining sources it is notated as a quaver. With the pedalling proposed by us here, and most probably intended by Chopin, the minim corresponds to the real duration of this note, tempering the sound of the parallel octaves $a\flat$-$a\flat^2$ and $g\flat$-$g\flat^2$ on the 2nd and 3rd beats.

Bars 29-30 L.H. The notation of the various sources:

As it is certain that none of these versions is correct, we give the most likely reconstruction of Chopin's notation.

Bar 31 R.H. The main text comes from **GC** (→**GE**) & **Kle**, the variant from **E**DM. There is no way of knowing how these discrepancies came about, and each version may be authentic.

Bar 32 This bar appears only in **E**DM. In the other extant sources the 1st quaver of bar 32 is followed by the 5 quavers of bar 33 and the work continues from bar 34. The authenticity of the version of **E**DM is supported by the following:
— the differentiation – despite their similarity – of bars 31 & 32; this rules out the possibility that the same bar may have been mistakenly written out twice in [**KC**] (→**E**DM) (dittography). The reverse error, meanwhile, namely the omission of one of two similar bars (haplography) may well have occurred in **GC**. Haplography occurred a number of times among copyists of Chopin's works (copies by Fontana of the *Preludes in G# minor*, Op. 28 No. 12, bars 78-79, and *in B♭*, Op. 28 No. 21, bar 54), and even with Chopin himself (autographs of the *Impromptu in C# minor*, WN 46, bars 121-122, and the *Sonata in B minor*, Op. 58, movt. IV, bars 175-176);
— the characteristically Chopinian textural device at the transition between bars 32 & 33 (a dyad as the melodic conclusion of the two preceding notes); such a deft detail makes the possible arbitrary interference of Kolberg very unlikely here (moreover, the addition here of a bar would be clearly the most far-reaching alteration that could be ascribed to Kolberg in either of the two *Polonaises* edited by him, *in B♭ minor*, WN 10, and *in G♭*, WN 35);
— the echo effect (*una corda*) employed in bars 33-34 sounds more natural when the juxtaposed passages of contrasting dynamics are of the same length (two bars each); generally, an even grouping of bars (2+4+4) is more natural in this section than an irregular grouping (2+3+4).

Bar 35 **GC** & **E**DM have here the meaningless term *alter mode* (**GC**) or *al ter moda* (**E**DM). This is certainly a misreading of the instruction to release the left pedal (*tre corde*), as it was interpreted in **GE**.

Bar 37 L.H. The main text comes from **GC** (→**GE**) & **Kle**, the variant from **E**DM. Both versions may be authentic, although mistakes or arbitrary changes made by copyists cannot be excluded.

Bar 38 L.H. The note $b\flat^1$ in the 1st chord appears in **GC** (→**GE**) & **Kle**.

p. 48

Bar 43 R.H. As the penultimate quaver **GC** (→**GE**) has the fourth $d\flat^1$-$g\flat^1$. The remaining sources have a third, as in bar 13. The error of **GC** is testified by the third in **GC'**, convergent with the remaining sources and with the analogous bar 13.

Bar 51 L.H. In the lower voice on the 2nd beat **GC** (→**GE**) erroneously has the fourth $g\flat$-$c\flat^1$.

Bar 56 R.H. As the last semiquaver on the 1st beat **GC** (→**GE**) has $c\flat^4$. The version of **GC'** ($e\flat^4$), convergent with the remaining sources and with the analogous bar 26, shows this to be a mistake by the copyist.

p. 49

Bars 58-59 The indication **Meno mosso** appears only in **E**DM. This edition is also the only one to give the term *Trio*, which always appears in Chopin *Polonaises* composed up to 1830.

Bar 61 & analog. R.H. The trill on the 3rd beat (our variant) appears in **E**DM & (in brackets) **Kle**. We cannot rule out here either arbitrary additions in [KC] (→**E**DM) & **Kle** or the omission of the ornament in **GC** (→**GE**).

Bar 62 & analog. R.H. The trill terminations are written out only in **E**DM.

Bars 66 & 117 L.H. Before the 2nd beat **E**DM has the grace note *f*, tied to the crotchet that follows it. The authenticity of this addition seems doubtful.

Bars 71-72 & 122-123 L.H. The accentuation of the bass notes and their extension to the value of a minim or crotchet are not consistently marked in the sources. In **GC** (→**GE**) & **Kle** the *a♭* in bars 71 & 122 is extended, and the other three bass notes (*g♭*, *a♭*, *g♭*) are accentuated. In **E**DM all the bass notes are extended, whilst accents appear on the *g♭* in bar 72 and all four notes in bars 122-123.

Bar 73 R.H. On the 3rd beat **E**DM has the rhythm ♪. ♬. The authenticity of this version seems doubtful, when we consider that in an analogous place (bar 124) this source gives yet another, doubtless arbitrary, version.

Bar 75 L.H. Missing on the 6th quaver in **GC** (→**GE**) is the note *g*.

p. 50

Bars 78 & 82 L.H. As the 1st note **E**DM has *F* in bar 78 and *G* in bar 82. This version, in which the third of the dominant placed in the bass is not immediately (on the 3rd beat) resolved in the following chord of the tonic, appears to be inauthentic. It presumably results from the alterations made by Kolberg in [KC].

Bar 83 R.H. As the hemidemisemiquaver ending the 1st beat **GC** (→**GE**) has only *d♭²*, whilst **EDM** & **Kle** have the third *b♭¹-d♭²*. Each of these versions may be authentic.

Bar 84 L.H. On the last quaver **GC** (→**GE**) & **Kle** have an additional *c♭¹*. We give the version of **EDM**, in which the doublings of the chord members do not appear until the ***f*** in the following bar.

Bar 86 L.H. The main text of the last quaver – the octave *A♭₁-A♭* – comes from **GC** (→**GE**) & **Kle**, the variant – the octave *A♭-a♭* – from **EDM**.

Bar 91 R.H. As the 1st quaver **GC** & **Kle** have the chord *e-g#-e¹-g#¹* (in **Kle** the note *e* is assigned to the L.H.). We give the unquestionably correct version of **EDM** & **GE**.

p. 51

Bar 95 R.H. The main text of the 1st quaver (*g#²*) comes from **EDM**, the variant (*g#³*) from **GC** (→**GE**) & **Kle**. One of the versions most probably results from a mistake in marking the scope of the *all'ottava* sign. We regard the leap of one octave (*g#²-g#¹*) as more natural in this context (cf. bars 93 & 97).
L.H. As the 2nd quaver **EDM** has the chord *g#-c#¹-e¹*. This anticipated entry of the C# minor chord (in relation to the melody and the change in the mood of the sound, specified by the term *dolce*) seems unnecessary. We adopt the version of **GC** (→**GE**) & **Kle**, which sounds more natural in this context.

Bar 98 L.H. The main text comes from **GC** (→**GE**) & **Kle**, the variant from **EDM**.

Bar 106 L.H. The main text comes from **GC** (→**GE**) & **Kle**. The slight variation in the 4th member of such a strict sequence (bars 100-107) is in keeping with Chopin's way of thinking, yet this version may also be erroneous (similarity to the following bar). The version given in the variant appears in **EDM**; one cannot rule out interference here by Kolberg.

Bar 108 L.H. At the beginning of the bar **EDM** has only the lower *E♭*. The octave appearing in the remaining sources links more naturally with the climax.

p. 52

Bar 110 R.H. The grace note *b♭²* before the 1st beat appears only in **EDM**. Analogies with the octave anacrusis at the beginning of the *Trio* and with the beginning of bar 67 reinforce the probability of this version being authentic.

Bar 116 R.H. In **GC** the note *g♭* in the chord on the 2nd beat is written unclearly, such that it is absent from **GE**.
R.H. In the chord on the 3rd beat **EDM** has the additional note *c♭¹*. This is either an error or one of Kolberg's additions.

Bar 122 L.H. On the 2nd quaver **EDM** has two semiquavers instead of the quaver. This is most probably an arbitrary change made by Kolberg. The last section of the *Trio* (bars 110-128) corresponds quite exactly to the first (bars 59-77) and in **[A]** was doubtless marked as its repeat. Thus all discrepancies between them result either from inaccurate reading or from later alterations.

Bar 124 R.H. In **EDM** the close of the bar has the following form:

. One may assume with a great degree of probability that this is an arbitrary change made by Kolberg (cf. previous comment). The transition from single notes to octaves that occurs both here and in the analogous bar 73 appears in a similar pattern, e.g., in the *Nocturne in E minor*, WN 23, bars 9-10.

Bar 127 R.H. Missing in **EDM** from the chords on the 3rd and 4th quavers is the note *e♭*. This is doubtless an error.

APPENDIX

(3). Polonaise in A flat major, WN 3. Earlier version

Sources – see commentary to main version of the *Polonaise*, p. 7.

Editorial principles
We give the version written in ink in **A**. We change enharmonically notes written contrary to the orthography. Editorial interventions are described in the comments to the main version, bars 1, 6, 13-38, 20, 23, 27-38, 40 & 44, 52-59 and 59.

p. 56

Bars 24-25 L.H. The chord in bar 24 initially had the value of a dotted minim and was repeated with the same rhythmic value in bar 25. We give the version corrected by Chopin already during the first phase of notating the work (in ink). It is not clear whether the slur over bar 24 related to the original version or was meant to suggest the need to sustain the sound of the chord in bar 24 after shortening – due to the R.H. passage – its rhythmic value.

p. 57

Bar 50 L.H. The third at the beginning of the bar initially had the value of a dotted minim.

(7). Polonaise in F minor, WN 12. Earlier version

Sources – see commentary to main version of the *Polonaise*, p. 13. The earlier version came into being in what was most probably a complete form as **[A1]**. The extant sources of this version – **AI** & **EF** – allow us to recreate it to a similar level of elaboration, although they do not give us the assurance that in particular places the adopted text corresponds exactly to the notation of the lost **[A1]**.

Editorial principles
We adopt as the base text **AI**, taking into account only those elements of **EF** (versions and performance markings) whose authenticity cannot be decidedly questioned. More specifically, we reject the probable misreadings of **AI** that appear in **EF**, the verbal and metronome tempo indications (cf. comment to *Polonaise in G# minor*, WN 4, bar 1), the ***mf*** signs and a large part of the pedal markings.

Performance markings appearing in **AI**: bars 1 & 48 ***p***, bar 16 accent above the *d♭²*, bar 49 ***pp***, bar 50 ***ppp***, bar 73 *espress.*, and also slurs in bars 5, 12, 13, 19 (*b¹-a♭³*), 26 (*c¹-c²*), 78 & 81-83.

p. 58

Bar 3 R.H. In **AI** the lower note of the last quaver, *f*, is assigned to the L.H. The version of **EF** represents a minor, but unquestionable improvement.

Bars 4-5 & 51 Instead of the ***mf*** appearing in **EF**, almost never used by Chopin, we give in parenthesis *espress.*, taken from **A2**.

Bar 14 L.H. At the beginning of the bar **GEF** erroneously has *G*.

Bars 15-18 & analog. L.H. The inner notes of the chords on the 5th quaver are absent from **EF**. The photocopy of **AI** available to the editors is not entirely legible here, but it seems more likely that these notes are written there (except for bar 18, which has the fourth *c¹-f¹*).

Bars 19-20 & analog. L.H. The main text is a corrected version of **AI**, the variant comes from **EF**. Read literally, the chord in **AI** sounds *c♭¹-f¹-a♭¹* (bar 20 is marked in short as a repeat of bar 19). However, the top two notes are tied with the *d¹-f¹* on the 2nd crotchet, which would indicate that Chopin meant them to be held. The text given by us sounds the same as the later version of **A2**, although it is written differently.

Bar 20 & analog. R.H. In **AI** bar 20 shows evidence of having been altered several times: it is possible to read two versions of the first two groups of semiquavers and three versions of the last. Most probably, Chopin began with the version given in the footnote, ultimately arriving at that which we adopt as the main text (concurrent with **A**2). Taking account of the variant of the last 4 semiquavers gives an intermediate version, the second in order of writing. In **EF** the corrected version of the beginning of the bar was combined with the original version of the ending:

Since this combination is doubtless due to Fontana being unaware of the order in which the versions were written in **A**I, we do not include it.

p. 59

Bar 23 ff. The possibly authentic fingering appears in **E**F (see comment to bar 78).

Bars 23-24 & analog. The arpeggios described in the footnote appear in **E**F.

Bars 23, 24 & analog. and 27 We replace the ***mf*** appearing in **E**F in bar 23 with *mezza voce* (in line with **A**2), which signifies practically the same and was used much more often by Chopin. By contrast, we take no account of two further, stylistically dubious, markings in **E**F: ***pp*** in bar 24 and another ***mf*** in bar 27.

Bar 26 L.H. Initially, the version of **EF**, , was most probably written also in **A**I, in which Chopin subsequently changed it to a version concurrent with **A**2 (without taking care to alter accordingly the rhythmic value of the opening *c*, leaving it as a minim). We give the later, clearly improved, version, shortening the value of the opening *c* – for clarity – to a dotted crotchet.

Bar 27 R.H. At the beginning of the bar **EF** has in the lower voice a quaver $e\flat^1$, tied to the grace note before it. This is doubtless an arbitrary alteration: both autographs have here 𝄾.
R.H. Missing in **A**I is the tie sustaining $e\flat^2$.

Bars 33-34 L.H. As the last strike (the 5th quaver of the bar) **E**F has in both bars the chord $b\flat$-f^1-$b\flat^1$. We give the version of **A**I, in which the $b\flat^1$ is deleted in both places.

p. 60

Bar 40 R.H. **E**F has a simplified, doubtless original, notation, which is lacking the sustained notes $b\flat^2$ on the 4th semiquaver and $e\flat^3$ on the 3rd quaver, as well as the separation of the upper voice on the 2nd beat.
L.H. We give the corrected version of **A**I. Originally, the first four quavers probably sounded there as follows: .
EF is concurrent with **A**I on the 1st and 3rd beats, but on the 3rd and 4th quavers has g-$b\flat$-$e\flat^1$ and $e\flat^1$-g^1. It is difficult to state whether this is just another version of Chopin's or the result of errors or editorial interference.

Bar 50 L.H. The main text comes from **A**I, the variant from **E**F. The version of **E**F is certainly authentic, and possibly even later. Such is indicated by the falling motion in thirds in the 2nd half of the bar, concurrent with the solution adopted in **A**2. The notation of **A**I is imprecise in this bar: missing are the chromatic signs, the rest and the dot extending the crotchet c^1.

Bars 51-72 In **A**I these bars are marked as a repeat (*Dal Segno*) of bars 5-26.

p. 62

Bars 73-80 In **A**I the repetition of these bars was not marked. This is certainly an inaccuracy of notation resulting from the working character of this manuscript.

Bar 78 R.H. Possibly authentic fingering appears only in **GE**F.

Bars 79-80 L.H. The tie sustaining $b\flat$ appears only in **A**I, the ties sustaining $a\flat$ and $e\flat$ only in **E**F. It seems impossible that Chopin could have such divergent concepts in this respect; most probably the notation of both sources is inexact. In assessing the possible authenticity of particular ties, we refer, among others, to the later version of **A**2, which raises no doubts. The following conclusions emerge:
— the tie sustaining $e\flat$ was overlooked in **A**I; it appears in **E**F & **A**2, and in making various changes to the other voices Chopin does not seem to have considered modifying the pedal point;
— in **E**F the tie sustaining $b\flat$ was overlooked or misread (as applying to the $a\flat$ – see below); in **A**2 this note is entirely absent from bar 80;
— the most doubts are raised by the tie sustaining $a\flat$: in **E**F it may have appeared due to a misreading from **A**I of the tie applying to $b\flat$, which is lacking the crotchet stem necessary for the precise marking of the hold; also, the presence of the tie in **A**2 does not testify its accidental omission from **A**I, as a number of other discrepancies between the autographs suggest that the difference in this detail may have been intentional.
For this reason, we give all three ties, leaving it to the performer to decide whether to take account of the tie sustaining $a\flat$.

Bar 80 (2. volta) R.H. The main text comes from **A**I, the variant from **E**F.

Bar 81 R.H. The second note of the sextuplet was initially written in **A**I (→**E**F) as b^1. Ultimately Chopin changed its notation to $c\flat^2$.

Bar 82 R.H. The grace note $d\flat^2$ after the turn appears only in **E**F. In analogous situations in other Chopin works we find versions both without a grace note (e.g. *Nocturne in E♭* Op. 9 No. 2, bar 26) and also with a grace note (e.g. *Nocturne in F# minor* Op. 48 No. 2, bars 41 & 103).
R.H. The main text and the variant are two ways of reading **A**I, in which the two versions appear on top of one another, such that we do not know which is later. **E**F has the version without a slur, **A**2 with the slur.

Bar 83 L.H. The version given in the footnote comes from **A**I, in which Chopin subsequently added the version given in the main text (concurrent with **A**2). However, he did not delete the previous version, possibly still unsure of its final conception. This caused a misreading of this bar in **E**F, in which the two versions were, so to speak, added together: .

Bar 85 The marking ***p*** appears only in **GE**F.

p. 63

Bars 88-89 L.H. **E**F does not have the notes $e\flat^2$ in the chords on the 3rd beat of bar 88 and the 1st beat of bar 89. This is probably a misreading of the unclear manuscript: in **A**I both chords are written an octave lower in the bass clef and are embraced by an *all'ottava* sign, such that the notes in question fall on the ledger lines. In such situations it is sometimes extremely difficult to establish the presence of notes within a chord in Chopin autographs, and doubts often arise (cf. comment to *Polonaise in B♭*, WN 17, bars 15 & 42).

Bar 90 L.H. The upper $e\flat^1$ in the chord on the 2nd beat appears only in **A**I.

Bars 91-98 In **A**I these bars are marked as a repeat (*Dal Segno*) of bars 73-80.

Bar 98 In **A**I the return of the main part of the *Polonaise* after the *Trio* was not marked, and in **E**F it is written out in full.

Jan Ekier
Paweł Kamiński